Resource Optimisation Through Environmental Leadership

Resource Optimisation Through Environmental Leadership

Group Captain **Manoj Kumar** VSM

Introduction by

Air Commodore **Jasjit Singh** AVSM, VrC, VM (Retd)

KNOWLEDGE WORLD
KW Publishers Pvt Ltd
New Delhi

in association with

Centre for Air Power Studies
New Delhi

2011 FPBA BEST PUBLISHERS AWARD (ENGLISH)

The Centre for Air Power Studies is an independent, non-profit, academic research institution established in 2002 under a registered Trust to undertake and promote policy-related research, study and discussion on the trends and developments in defence and military issues, especially air power and the aerospace arena, for civil and military purposes. Its publications seek to expand and deepen the understanding of defence, military power, air power and aerospace issues without necessarily reflecting the views of any institution or individuals except those of the authors.

Jasjit Singh
Director General
Centre for Air Power Studies
P-284, Arjan Path
Subroto Park
New Delhi 110010

Tele: (91-11) 25699131
E-mail: diroffice@aerospaceindia.org

Published in India by
Kalpana Shukla
KW Publishers Pvt Ltd
4676/21, First Floor, Ansari Road, Daryaganj, New Delhi 110002
T: +91.11.23263498 /43528107 E: knowledgeworld@vsnl.net | www.kwpub.com

ISBN 978-93-81904-24-4

Printed and bound in India

This book is dedicated to:

The earliest memories of my childhood when as a care-free child I used to venture out in the small town where my father was posted; to be one with nature, enjoying its pristine, raw beauty; playing with the wind in my face; climbing trees; jumping in the pond used for irrigation, with gay abandon; eating homemade butter made from the milk from cows reared at home.

And now a witness to the concrete structure that stands where the trees used to be, with air-conditioners installed to provide the comforts that nature had provided; such pleasures of a simple, independent life our children may never know.

Contents

Acknowledgements

It is normally a pleasantly arduous task to write a book and this was my third in the Centre for Air Power Studies (CAPS). The first book was a joint UNEP-CAPS publication *'Toolkit for Defence Forces'* for management of ozone depleting substances; the second book on *'Environment Change and National Security'* explored the linkages between security and environmental issues. The present work on optimisation of resources treats the subject of environment from a different angle. While writing on 'environment and the military' has been personally satisfying, the road has not been easy. The organisations that deal with environmental and defence services in India are yet to take cognizance of the mutual interactions that exist other than mere disaster relief operations undertaken by the military. In this background, as a serving military officer, to be allowed to explore the depth of the subject was an opportunity that came my way due to the strategic vision of the Director General CAPS, Air Commodore Jasjit Singh.

I had many fruitful discussions with the faculty at CAPS, which helped me improve my work; what stood out were the frank and bold thoughts from Air Marshal AK Singh, Distinguished Fellow at CAPS that helped me resolve many contradictions in the thought process. My two meetings with the Special Secretary Shri JM Mauskar in the Ministry of Environment and Forests (MoEF) also provided me with a different perspective on the subject.

At each stage I received the full support of top Indian Air Force (IAF) hierarchy in the form of granting interviews, discussing ideas or permission to visit AF stations for collecting primary data. I am thankful to the Air Officer Commanding-in-Chief, Western Air Command (AOC-in-C, WAC) (now the Vice Chief of Air Staff - VCAS) Air Marshal DC Kumaria, Deputy Chief of the Air Staff (DCAS) Air Marshal RK Sharma, and the Senior Maintenance Staff Officer (SMSO), WAC (now Air Officer in-charge Maintenance - AOM) Air Marshal P Kanakraj, Air Vice Marshal Amit Aneja, Air Vice Marshal NK Tandon and Air Commodore MS Shekhawat, for their valuable guidance and support. Many value additions to my work were made by Air Vice Marshal Kapil Kak, former Additional Director, CAPS and I am thankful to him for the same.

The international discourse on environment change is evolving fast. With the carbon emission-cap likely to be faced after 2020, the impacts that would be felt by the governmental departments (including the military) in India need serious analysis. As already mentioned above, this subject is in its infancy within the military and I was fortunate to receive the support of Ms Dhanasree Jayaram (now in CAPS) who helped me fine-tune the work by being a valuable source of information.

The discourse presented in the book also benefited from discussions that I had with knowledgeable persons like Dr Stephen Andersen (formerly of the US EPA), noted writer Ms Cleo Pascal, my friend and guide Dr Gopichandran, and Mr Atul Bagai of the UNEP. The balance and counter-balance process that is essential while writing a treatise like the present one is honed when one interacts with people with a wide global perspective. I am thankful to all these persons for giving me an insight into their thought process.

The well stocked library at CAPS was of great help and its extremely helpful staff went out of the way to make available material even from other libraries for undertaking research on the subject.

The team of KW Publishers who undertook the compilation and editing of the book deserves special mention here. Their meticulousness became evident as they observed even small mistakes in the work and efficiently ironed out the rough patches.

I have reserved my special thanks and reverences for my parents who have ingrained in me a system of valuing and conserving resources. This was the prime reason that the subject appealed to me.

My wife stood by me with words of encouragement whenever she found the mood turning intense and sceptical. Thank you, Preeti! My sons, Varun and Ytharth insist that they deserve recognition for allowing me to work peacefully without any major heart-stoppers and I agree with them.

Toward Environmental Leadership: An Introductory Essay

Jasjit Singh

> What is a good disciple?
> A master in the making.
> What is a master?
> A successful disciple.
> — Mooji, A Renowned Thinker and Author

Military organisations around the globe are constantly evolving and transforming to stay ahead of their potential adversaries. The transformational processes are largely technology-driven, with the human resource also evolving commensurately. Control of cutting edge technology is, therefore, a huge advantage for any military. A new paradigm gets added to the canvas when such technologies and evolved processes result in reduced use of resources, to achieve a relatively 'tail-free' operation. Since the goal of a military organisation is to always increase the 'tooth-to-tail' ratio for enhancing the punch, optimisation of resource consumption gives them the necessary leverage to do so. In the process of reducing its dependence on resources, if an organisation also manages to decrease its environmental footprint, then it can only be termed as a win-win situation – both for society and for the organisation. This may seem a very desirable outcome of the resource optimisation foray but the process requires a bold and informed leadership that possesses deep insight into the way the organisation works; also the answer to the question of what constitutes environmentally friendly activities within a military organisation should be clear to an environment leader.

Air Commodore **Jasjit Singh** AVSM VrC VM, awarded the Padma Bhushan by the President of India in 2006 for a life-time's contribution to national security and defence, is the Director General, Centre for Air Power Studies, New Delhi.

What constitutes a resource? Any input that an organisation needs for its operation would be called a resource. This, in turn, presents an opportunity to fine-tune procedures that would allow more to be achieved from the same input. The fine-tuning procedures are applied across a wide spectrum of activities that the organisation undertakes. Specifically for a military organisation, armament consumption during training and operations is a basic necessity; it is also a major source of the military's environmental footprint. Optimising its usage would be highly desirable for enhancing the military's effectiveness albeit it is a challenge because its usage is different from that of any other resource used by an organisation. This, probably, is the only resource whose consumption in the military, for training or in war, would attract accolades and not adverse comments. Even then, optimising its consumption to enhance the efficiency quotient of usage – to obtain higher value from its consumption – can only be termed as environmental leadership. The challenge to optimise usage of such a resource was duly recognised and the good practices that have been suggested in this book may be used to achieve higher standards of armament inventory management. A civil organisation can also draw a parallel as the inventory optimisation practices suggested herein have sound principles of management as their backbone.

While consumption of resources is a must for organisations to be able to have some output, it is also essential that waste is reduced to the bare minimum, thereby leading to optimum consumption. Waste management plays an important part in providing a healthy environment to the inhabitant of a military formation. This, in turn, acts as a motivator for the troops located therein to voluntarily put their best foot forward. More importantly, it also has the potential to provide feedback to the audit authorities about the avenues where resources are not being optimally utilised. An inordinately high amount of industrial waste is a pointer towards processes not being run as per their original design. An environmental auditing system is designed to take care of assessing the two-way interaction between the infrastructure and the environment. While the impact of inefficient use of resources on the working of the military formation needs to be judged, it is also essential to observe the effects that it has on the environment. This is because a degraded environment would have an equally adverse impact on the working of the formation and on the human resources. A military leader would definitely guard against such prospects and, thus, it is essential that the environmental impact of actions being undertaken is studied by them. A waste management study would also reveal how standardised good practices of municipal and industrial waste disposal systems can be incorporated in the audit process of the organisation.

The audit process in the military has a great potential to provide feedback to the commanders, which should allow far-reaching changes, provided the scope of the audit is expanded with adequate training of the auditors. The importance of the process is apparent from the fact that it even allows correction of policies and their implementation, which would result in enhanced effectiveness of a complete and well integrated system. Environmental audits form an important part of the EMS (Environment Management System). In all audit systems, it is beneficial to work with quantitative benchmarks. Developing such benchmarks for environmental audit is rightly the first step that any organisation should take. It is not an easy beginning as inventory mapping for processes that have an impact on the environment is normally not a priority for many organisations and it would require a visionary to realise the positive fall-out of undertaking such an activity. Once inventory mapping has been accomplished, setting quantitative benchmarks for the purpose of audits becomes easier. A periodical comparison of these figures would highlight the efficiency/deficiency in the implementation or in the need for introducing new processes. This becomes possible once the top hierarchy has a positive orientation towards fostering a resource efficient culture within the organisation with a healthy environment as a welcome consequence.

Resources can only be optimised when their usage is astutely planned at the procurement stage itself. In other words the optimisation process begins even before the resources are available in the organisation. Defence procurement has been much in debate in the media in the last few years. The procurement procedures have been modified and refined over the years. It is appreciated that satisfaction of all parties is difficult in a system as complex as the Indian defence organisation. However, it is heartening to note that Life Cycle Cost (LCC) has been recognised as an important attribute of comparative bid analysis. Organisationally it is now being given due importance in the Ministry of Defence (MoD) and within the Service Headquarters (HQ) too. This needs to become a pan-organisation initiative so as to ensure that resource planning is carried out at the time of procurement itself. A product that is recyclable or has the potential for life extension needs this to be factored positively in the costing process and thereby in the comparative analysis, even if the initial capital costs are higher. This analysis has the capacity to alter the way product costing is done and needs to be well understood for increasing the effectiveness of scarce resources being spent. LCC is an important criterion that has to become a norm in all procurement decisions as it considers the product across the entire spectrum of its operational life and even after. It is important as, by placing a premium on the usability of the product over a long time span, its optimisation is automatically ensured.

Since cost-cutting cannot be in exchange for lowering the operational edge, it is essential that alternatives already mentioned like life extension and recycling are positively considered during the procurement process. Another way to do so would be to go in for a high amount of indigenisation. Any military that manages to retain the technological edge by sourcing indigenous products would obviously enjoy prolonged and consistent support. With the defence budget under pressure everywhere, it would be essential to save costs wherever possible and utilise these savings for Research and Development (R&D) endeavours; a closed loop system that allows greater focus on research, design and development of technologies, should be a priority for leaders of any organisation. This fits in well with the initiative of reducing the military's environmental footprint. With the military technology being intrinsically complex – and air power technology more so – an additional focus is required on the related field of technological maturity of the recipient organisation, to be able to absorb products developed with the cradle-to-cradle approach. The cradle-to-cradle approach to design and development is becoming common in cutting edge technology, primarily due to cost competitiveness and environmental considerations.

The Future Unfolds

The story of our mastery over critical defence technologies is that of perennial under-achievement. Even with a higher science education system that till recently was the cynosure of the world, India has been consistently lagging behind the rest of its competitors. A detailed analysis of the current state of affairs would reveal two fundamental reasons for this: (i) the reality of deindustrialisation that was imposed on India by colonialism which stood as the world's second largest manufacturer in the early 18th century (with only China slightly ahead of India); (ii) the developed world having access to the Industrial Revolution, took advantage of countries like India that could not and, hence, the former moved far ahead. Lack of industrialisation till independence also led to lack of understanding that had a negative effect even where opportunities existed for better performance. Too many mistakes were made; and progress has been overly slow. As a consequence of the historical realities, highly trained engineers and scientists from premier institutes either leave for greener pastures abroad or find jobs that are high paying such as in the financial sector or in management consultancy firms. Alternatively, they would seek power in the corridors of the Indian bureaucracy/police services. The minority that stays back in the field of research finds that there is hardly any demand for them from the government or the industry to prove themselves, since there is not much appreciation – monetarily or otherwise – accorded in this field. With the confluence of green and military technology like Nanotechnology (NT) or those using Rare Earth Elements (REE), a new technology world order is emerging. For the non-achievers in this order, it would mark an extension of technology denial regimes by adding to the existing barriers to transfer of Green Technology (GT). These barriers exist currently in the form of Intellectual Property Rights (IPR) and funding mechanisms for GT transfers. The nation that manages to master 'confluence technologies' would benefit doubly. On the one hand, there are endless possibilities where these technologies can be used to provide an edge in the civil and military domains and, on the other, they would reduce consumption of resources due to the essential nature of this technology to produce sustained output. It is, thus, extremely important that investments in such technologies are considered the highest priority through different routes of development and technology transfers.

With tangible progress in techno-industrialisation and the higher education system, a new paradigm has emerged as the government, prodded by the media and the judiciary, tries to bring in more transparency in its operations. Various organs of the government, including the military, have to display positive action on this front. This has necessitated inculcation of a different skill set in the military leaders. The new set of skills required now has to focus on better understanding of the civil system and has to be able to develop communication skills that portray organisational requirements succinctly. The training programmes within the military have to be suitably modified to prepare future leaders for dealing with many so-called civil subjects like environmental regulations, media management, etc, which have an overarching connect with military functioning. Many years ago, the military was not entirely on board when India became a signatory to the Montreal Protocol that has been used to prevent proliferation of Ozone Depleting Substances (ODS). These substances were (and are) being widely used within the military for mission critical uses and even then, the impact of their absence was not studied. The military hierarchy was not even aware of such an agreement being inked, thus, remaining ignorant of its impacts. Such a situation may be repeated once India has to comply with carbon emissions cap norms post 2020. The military being an important stakeholder in the affair, may again find itself under-prepared if the planning process doesn't start for suitable modification in its functioning. In this context, the training and orientation of the future leaders on this changed social dynamics acquire great significance. This book has gone beyond just making the leaders aware of the oncoming changes: it lays down in detail, the syllabus of training programmes that may be created at various levels, for preparing the organisation to deal with them. This is a very important beginning to ensure that vital resources do not get wasted when certain restrictions are placed in the future, apparently in compliance with India's international commitments. Another important aspect that would require attention is for the defence organisation to be proactive and not just accept such restrictions perfunctorily. The military leaders have to articulate their concerns at appropriate levels of the government now, even when they are not considered party to such deliberations at this juncture. Being left out of the decision-making on such crucial policies may prove counter-productive at a later date as was the case in respect of restrictions on ODS production consequent to the Montreal Protocol.

On a related subject of civil-military juxtaposition, the need is greater than ever for the military to manage the media effectively and wisely. Such demands would arise in the near future and they would become specially challenging during operations/hostilities. The events of 2012 have marked a low hitherto unseen, in the image of our Army in particular and the defence organisation in general. Expecting a military leader to be suddenly prepared to handle the media just because of his/her seniority is leaving the door open for controversies. Preparing the leaders consciously to be able to take on such responsibilities is the need of the hour. The Ministry of Defence also needs to play its part in ensuring that its working is transparent and engagement with the public, the media and the industry, is well coordinated.

It is in the above context that Group Captain Manoj Kumar has carried out extensive research into the issues noted above and much more over the past two years. This is an outstanding study, and even unique in many ways, by which the professional military reader would be able to enhance his/her professional abilities into new dimensions which most of the old timers have generally stayed away from. The issues covered in this volume point the way into the future, a future we often ignore till it becomes the present, by which time it is too late to alter the environment. I was privileged to read the book as it evolved and am now writing to strongly urge the military people, the civil service, academics and laymen to read it and imbibe the central thrust for a policy for the future.

1

New Frontiers of Military Leadership: Environmental Forays

Environmental Leadership

Traditionally, the role of the military has been envisaged to safeguard the country's borders – air, land and sea. It is rarely, if at all, that the common populace gets to see the social face of the military monolith of their country. This happens whenever there is a natural calamity and the governments – provincial or federal – are overwhelmed. The military then interacts with its civil counterparts and earns lavish praise for securing the affected population from the elements. As nature turns benign again, the military retracts till the time such an eventuality recurs. This '*on and off*' facet of military-social interactions is being seen with growing regularity as sudden climatic events are visiting us with increasing frequency. Rarely do these instances of demonstrated military professionalism, discipline and leadership get etched in the memory of the country's inhabitants. As nature's fury abates, the people's memory also fades. Thus, an important facet of military social leadership never emerges from the shadows.

The senior echelons of the Indian Army take pride, and justly so, in protecting the endangered ecology of many difficult terrains by the use of their Eco Territorial Army Battalions[1]. Planting of trees and thereafter maintaining them is a noble and traditional way of protecting the environment. However, there are many arguments for and against involving the military's decision-making body in this pursuit as it is not its primary objective. Planting trees also does not have an effect on the pursuit of any military objective. This evident lack of clarity and focus on the matter has put a stop to the expansion of the scope of the process to the other two Services i.e. the Indian Air Force

(IAF) and the Indian Navy (IN). Therefore, such forays by the Indian Army have not mirrored its leadership role in the social sector of environment protection, to be emulated by the other two Services. The questions that arise from the observations mentioned above are:

- How does one define leadership in the social domain within the military? What are the various facets of this form of leadership that the military can demonstrate? What purpose would such demonstration serve for the military?
- Is there a need for the leadership in the Indian military to be seized of the matters of the environment and should they even consider these issues in their decision-making calculus?
- The pertinent question is whether environmental leadership in the military is any different from similar abilities of other organisations?
- What actions on the part of the Indian military could be considered as demonstration of leadership in protection of the environment?

This chapter, with a focus on the IAF, would attempt to answer the core issues of the first three questions posed above. Further, an attempt would be made to answer the last and the most difficult question posed on how this leadership process can be carried forward by actual implementation that would help the IAF to convert environmental forays into an opportunity to become more resource efficient.

Traditional versus Environmental Leadership

There are many definitions of leadership by experts, with striking similarities. Some *traits* of leaders like drive, desire to lead, integrity, self-confidence, intelligence, and domain knowledge have been considered important enough to merit almost a ubiquitous mention wherever elements of leadership are discussed. Similarly, a few experts have focussed entirely on the interpersonal relations or team-building abilities of a leader. They define leadership as an ability to influence the interpersonal relationships towards achievement of predefined objectives or goals. The question then arises as to why should a separate entity of environmental leadership be carved out? It is natural to question whether environmental leadership is a broader concept and not contained within the well defined allegory of leadership.

A contemporary environment leader does not necessarily fit the bill of traditional leaders like Mahatma Gandhi, Churchill, Mandela and many other greats of yore. These great leaders had the ability to carry the nation with them (and probably most of the globe). Not many environmental leaders can hope to achieve such heights, considering the fractured state of the debate. In most cases, our knowledge of the environment is littered with contradictions, and facts are difficult to master. The cause and effect paradigms do not always seem to converge. It would seem that in such a scenario, it would be highly improbable to locate a person with domain knowledge of the environment along with the ability to 'motivate the interpersonal relationships'. This is where an environmental leader is different from a traditional leader. An environmental leader is more of an epitome of personal drives, who works in the area of unknowns. As in an ecosystem, the boundaries are permeable, with matter and energy changing forms, an environment leader learns to work not only within but also outside the boundaries of the defined systems and paradigms, his own or those of the society. The boundaries that are imposed by history, geographical features, human institutions and jurisdiction, probably present the biggest challenge to a leader working towards improving the environment. To overcome this challenge, a traditional leader would work towards redefining these boundaries in line with the aspiration of his/her followers and his own beliefs; however, this approach may be redundant in matters of the environment. A classic example in this case is that of management of Ozone Depleting Substances (ODS) under the Montreal Protocol. The ODS banned under the protocol are being phased out and are required to be replaced by chemicals with a lower Ozone Depleting Potential (ODP). While moving to redefine this boundary, it was realised that the envisaged replacements of a few of these chemicals have a very significant global warming potential, such as Hydro Fluorocarbons (HFCs) for Chlorofluorocarbons/Hydro Chlorofluorocarbons (CFCs/HCFCs), are capable of causing great harm to the environment due to their greenhouse effect. Thus, redefining boundaries is not always a suitable approach in environmental matters. *Working across boundaries rather than redefining them is an essential attribute to be possessed by an environmental leader.*

It must have been noted by now that one of the most distinguishing facets of an environmental leader would be that it is an acquired mindset and ability. However, its prerequisite would be the possession of a vision as well as the ability to go beyond a value system. A major challenge that is normally faced by leaders is that of *uncertainty*. In environmental issues, this is paramount in its manifestation. Not only the future but even the history of environment change is being constantly debated and is still rather uncertain. When faced with such an opaque scenario, a cynical attitude would normally appear in weaker personalities. A leader has to dispel this thought process, first in himself and then in his followers and even in the naysayer.

The complexity of our ecosystem, coupled with the fact that the elements remain an enigma for even the greatest brains of our times, poses another challenge to the leaders. With limited know-how at one's disposal, it is an onerous task to be able to convince and lead the masses towards a safer habitat. The belief in the simplicity of actions that transcend science and are observed in the region of common sense, is of utmost importance. The adage that 'you can't manage what you don't understand' is a thing of the past for an environmental leader. Managing change, much more than what the corporate 'change management' has taught, is an imperative for an environmental leader. The incredulity of the words 'what you don't understand, you can't be doing' is lost on such a leader. Working with the convergence of uncertainty, changes, boundaryless systems and an urgent need for actions can be observed in an environmental leader.

After explaining various attributes that go into the making of an environmental leader, a definition may be attempted. **Environmental leaders are those who can define environmental problems by rising above their own value system and in the face of an uncertain, seamless environmental complexity, are able to carry hard decisions to their logical conclusions, with willing actions from their followers.** It is worth mentioning here that an environmental leader has to possess the ability to be able to rise above his/her beliefs and think of the global commons. It is a very intrinsic process, fairly ordinary and simple for the human psyche, and as an oxymoron, thereby, not easily achievable. This would be explained in little more detail and with specific examples when the issues of military leadership in environmental matters are discussed.

Environmental Issues: Involvement of the Military

Before we discuss the environmental leadership issues that the military may need to imbibe, it would be prudent to consider the drivers for the military to make forays in this, primarily, social domain. Environment protection has long been seen as a subject that merits attention by the social leadership. The Indian military establishment has remained aloof, almost a bystander to the 'mitigation and adaptation' debate ranging around them. It has always been felt that regulations and policies on the environment are concerned with the ways of life that touch such social issues like pollution, forestry, land use, and energy conservation, etc. The security implications of environment change and, more importantly, the contribution of the military during their peace-time role towards jeopardising the environment, have not been visualised[2]. The military has many serious issues of national security to ponder upon and an issue of social security such as environment protection obviously does not really count as a priority for them. These impediments to adopting environmental leadership would be considered later in the chapter. However, it would be sensible to add here that this is not because of any adverse intentions on their part but due to the gap that exists in understanding the favourable consequences of adopting environmentally sound processes in military operations.

Environmentally sound processes imply those procedures and systems that would be resource-efficient, thereby, cost-effective and overall easier to manage and control. These applications have a very large canvas. From a mundane activity such as waste disposal in a military installation to operational scenarios demanding optimum utilisation of fossil fuel and armaments, figuratively speaking, the field of vision is, therefore, 360 degrees. Some of these optimum procedures would have been implemented by the military organisations on their own, considering their efficacy. However, defining their environmentally sound implications would impress upon the military hierarchy that their implementation is essential from more angles than one. It is a win-win situation if their implementation actually results in an operationally stronger military organisation. This is the intention in defining these processes and describing as to how they can be made more resource efficient.

Military leadership would be truly demonstrated if they were to achieve not only the 'low hanging fruits' but also consider activities that demand bold and 'out of the box' actions. If a military commander is to carry out an energy efficiency and conservation study in his/her installation in India, he would most likely face the derision of his subordinates and superiors alike. However, if by implementing the recommendation of the same study, it is demonstrated that the formation had been able to cut the reaction time for deployment and also achieve cost cuts, the commander is likely to be lauded for the effort. This is not a trodden road for the Indian military but one which would have to be traversed often, considering, the needs of the present times.

As already mentioned, the canvas of the correctly managed, environmentally sound procedures is very large. Therefore, a representative sample of the subjects that are proposed to be covered are mentioned below:

- Resources Management: Armament Inventory.
- Review of Technology Transfer and Procurement Procedures.
- Energy Conservation and Efficiency.
- Waste Management.
- Environmental Training in the IAF
- Environmental Audit

} In a typical IAF formation

Environmental Leadership in the Military

After having defined the requirements for environmental leadership, it is appropriate **to define the necessity to introduce such leadership, at the desired levels of the military hierarchy**. The process involved in this inculcation process would be covered separately when the training aspects are covered.

Militaries in most of the developing countries are not yet actively taking adequate steps to address environment change. The social tag attached to the subject has proved to be a hindrance for it to be considered by the military hierarchy. Since its correlation with military matters has not been studied, it has not been emphasised upon sufficiently. The developed countries, on the other hand, have been actively focussing on the subject of carbon mitigation for quite some time. It started due to their respective governments' regulations requiring their departments to be compliant of energy and resource efficiency initiatives. Once the processes got optimised in line with the government's regulations, it was soon realised that the operational efficiency was a welcome byproduct of such endeavours. With this realisation, a serious investigation of these issues was started by the top echelons of these militaries. Consider the policy issued on the subject by the US Army given below:

Box 1[3]

The Army Strategy for the Environment

"Sustain the Mission – Secure the Future"

The United States Army has long recognised that our mission is only accomplished because America entrusts us with its most precious resources – its sons and daughters. It is our obligation to ensure that our soldiers today – and the soldiers of the future – have the land, water, and air resources they need to train; a healthy environment in which to live; and the support of local communities and the American people.

The new Army Strategy for the Environment: Sustain the Mission – Secure the Future establishes a long-range vision that enables the Army to meet its mission today and into the future. Sustainability is the foundation for this strategy and a paradigm that focuses our thinking to address both present and future needs while strengthening community partnerships that improve our ability to organise, equip, train, and deploy our soldiers as part of the joint force.

Sustainability connects our activities today to those of tomorrow with sound business and environmental practices. We have learned over the past decades that simply complying with environmental regulations will not ensure that we will be able to sustain our mission. We must strive to become systems thinkers if we are to benefit from the interrelationships of the triple bottom line of sustainability: mission, environment, and community. To sustain the future Army, we must implement effective policies and practices that safeguard the environment and our quality of life in a manner that our nation expects of us.

The Army Strategy for the Environment does not pretend to dictate all the answers. It is only the starting point that commits Army leaders at all levels to certain goals and challenges them to develop innovative methods to achieve these goals. Achieving the vision outlined in this strategy will require a deep and personal commitment from every member of the Army team – every leader, every soldier, every civilian, and every family member. For the Army to be successful on its quest toward sustainability, we must all do our part to Sustain the Mission, Secure the Future!

-sd-	-sd-
Peter J. Schoomaker	R.L. Brownlee
General, United States Army	Acting Secretary of the Army
Chief of Staff	

It is clear from the policy statement mentioned here that the US Army is actively taking into account mission accomplishment on the same page as environment protection. This throws open a new vista in perspective planning that is done by the Service Headquarters (HQ) in India. The focus on the community-military partnership, individual soldier, and, most importantly, the need to sustain future missions by following environmentally apt practices, does require a deep understanding of the interactions of the environment with military working. The sustainability approach needs to be followed for 'military' reasons, as different from purely social ones. This is the crux of environmental leadership in the military. Broadly, the objectives and benefits of demonstrating environmental leadership in the military are given below:

- ***Strengthen Operational Efficiency***

Following sustainable practices is bound to result in reduced dependence on fossil fuels, scarce resources, and energy. This has a cascading effect upon reducing the military's logistics tail during operations and training and on the cost of missions. With the reduced costs, the military would have more resources on its hands to deploy in priority areas of enhanced training levels and quality of life. Reduced logistics signature is also an operationally desirable feature of any military mission. This does not expose their vulnerabilities and is, thus, a much sought-after attribute by the military planners. To be able to deploy/move fast with least encumbrances and being less dependent on worries related to availability of energy are achievable elements of sustainable mission planning.

- ***Innovative Process***

To reduce dependence on energy and resources, innovation in thinking and technology is essential. Militaries are normally committed to technological innovations as that gives them an edge over their potential adversaries. However, extending this commitment to innovative resource planning is a requirement of environmental leadership. Ensuring introduction of energy efficient processes, renewable sources of energy, and energy and resource conservation (as different from pure efficiency measures) methods would reduce costs while protecting human life and the environment. It would call for consulting professionals who have domain know-how and also the relevant sectors of both government and private enterprises. This would result in commensurate benefits in expanding the scientific and technological base that would ensure buffering the military organisation from fast pace changes in these fields and allow it to remain potent and ahead. As an example, for captive power sources for communication equipment of the military, a change from diesel-based power generation to renewable energy sources may result in savings and operational benefits that are being mentioned here. Such opportunities exist in many facets of military operations; the requirement is to invest in commitment to innovative thinking. This is only possible if the military leadership is convinced of the process and its benefits. Showcasing environmental leadership is of the essence here.

- ***Enhance Quality of Life***

A safe and healthy environment is a sure recipe for a good quality of life, one that all of us aspire for. Military formations are inextricably connected to the local community that in a way sustains it. Whether deployed in a remote location or operating from a peace location, an air force formation undertakes operations that have an impact on the local community. From disposal of used Fuel, Oil and Lubricants (FOL) to lead contamination of ground water from the small arms firing ranges, all such activities would harm the health of not only the soldiers but also their families and the supporting local community. Environmental leadership within the military would enhance the knowledge of such actions, leading to empathy and, thus, support for innovative ideas on recycling and waste disposal. The close and collaborative nature of relations between the local community and military formation becomes a potential game-changer at the time of actual operations. India has learnt this very well during the wars (including that of Kargil) that it had to fight. Since the military is already a source of leadership and inspiration for the masses, it is important that it treats this feature of community interaction with the necessary impetus that it deserves.

- ***Sustainability Ethos***

A military that adopts sustainability in its ethos would have a strategic advantage as it would be able to adapt to changes much faster than one that doesn't. This advantage would be derived from the conditioning of its personnel in adopting a parsimonious approach towards utilisation of resources. Such a military organisation would also derive the respect of the nation and international acclaim. To inculcate the sustainability ethos, it would be essential for the leadership to introduce the reality of safeguarding the planet and their nation – in that order – to their personnel. This process would be covered in more detail when the training procedures required in doing so are dealt with.

It is essential to develop a sustainability ethos within the military as more and more conflicts in this world would take place due to dearth of resources. If the military organisations are going to further add to these scarcities, then the country would be caught in a downward spiral even as it tries to meet all possible requirements of its military that are as it is considered sacrosanct in most countries. The important aspect to watch out for in the process of optimisation is that at no stage should the operational readiness of the military get adversely affected. Building efficiency through environmental audits and ingraining of a sustainability ethos is a possible way out. If the military can do more training at lower costs, it would benefit as also the country.

- ***Minimise Total and Life Cycle Costs (LCCs)***

Although this requirement of low cost inputs is an important part of the environmental leadership and sustainability ethos, it is being mentioned separately, primarily to lend additional focus to the issue. Costs that are obvious are the ones that easily attract attention. For example, consider a hypothetical case wherein the cost of FOL at one of the border bases of the Indian Air Force would be almost the same as in a peace location in another state, barring a little variation in taxes, etc. However, this would not take into account the costs involved – in monetary and environmental terms – for transporting the stores by the IAF aircraft/vehicles to the point of dispersion. This is also known as fully burdened cost of FOL. The environmental costs would further get exacerbated if one takes into consideration the fact that owing to the remote location of this base, it may not have a proper disposal system for the used FOL, leading to unsafe disposal and thereby causing contamination of ground water.

In the same context, the life cycle costs of any military hardware may be much more than the capital cost of its procurement. The costs involved in carrying out preventive maintenance add to the total cost of operations of military hardware. These costs include ease of maintenance, its frequency, parts change and transportation of these parts to and from the repair agency, their repair/maintenance, additional hardware or float needed to ensure the numbers available do not deplete below a certain limit (lest it affects the national security) and deployment of additional personnel to take care of these processes. Most of these costs are hidden and not accounted for when one calculates resource efficiency. This may induce a false sense of complacency due to inaccurate costing analysis and, thus, present an inaccurate picture.

Military's Environmental Strategy

This debate now enters a crucial phase and brings us to the question of **how to define the strategy on environmental leadership that has to be adopted by the military?** Although the question may seem complex, the solution is simple as is the case with most of nature's creation. **The environmental strategy of the military can be defined as the optimisation of processes**

that are capable of ushering in the future at less comprehensive costs (environmental and life cycle), combined with higher operational capability. The words that need to be tagged here are 'processes', 'costs' and 'present-future' juxtaposition.

Processes that would have an impact on environmental costs and operational capability of the military organisation would differ as per the operating conditions. Certainly, the training methodology, maintenance procedures, inventory planning and management, and estate management are a few of the subjects that have an impact on operational readiness as well as the environmental signatures of the organisation. Their optimisation can be achieved if one considers – and is willing to decrease – the cost of operations. In the US, pushed by federal legislative mandates and by the need to save money on energy costs, the US Navy has reduced its overall traditional energy consumption level by 12 percent as of 2008 with projects centred around wind energy generation, solar photovoltaic systems, geothermal systems, and ocean thermal energy conversion.[4] Since the legislations demanded and the need of the hour (due to economic downturn) was such that these processes had to be introduced in the developed countries, the Indian military now needs to demonstrate proactive strategy and be a role model for other similarly placed governmental and non-governmental organisations, in the national and international arenas.

Inventory mapping of the processes is normally the first step towards their optimisation. The US military spent $20 billion in 2008, consuming 4 billion gallons of jet fuel, 220 million gallons of diesel and 73 million gallons of gasoline.[5] Till such figures are compiled and compared on a year-on-year basis, a need would not be felt to engage in the optimisation process. The leadership would be seized of the matter only once the potential for making wholesome changes is seen. An environmental leader creates the opportunity by visualising these avenues. Any reduction in energy inputs, either by conservation or conversion to renewable sources has a cascading effect on reducing the dependence on a particular source – leading to energy security. This, in turn, allows for greater operational flexibility, reduced reaction time – a necessity for any military – and energy security. This becomes more and more important for operations in remote areas. Consider the following news article of a solar powered railway station published in *The Times of India*, New Delhi edition, on January 27, 2010.

Box 2

India gets 1st green Rly station
New Delhi: Railways has inaugurated India's first green station at Manwal on the Jammu-Udhampur rail route.

With the tiny station facing frequent power cuts, it has been a provided a supply of solar power. "A request was made to J&K SEB for providing reliable electric power supply to this station...it was planned to generate onsite renewable energy through solar panels," said A. S. Negi, spokesperson, Northern Railway.

Sources said that now station lighting and fans are working on solar power. The state electric supply is a standby source, which can be used in case of any failure of the solar system. Electric load of S&T installations and one water cooler is on state electric supply. Additional solar panels for increasing backup for power supply and standalone lights for complete platform lighting are planned to be provided for further improvement in the system after the trials are successful.

To reduce the existing load at the small station, some surplus fittings have been removed and energy efficient T-5 fittings, 60W fans, new exhaust fans (55 Watt) and CFLs have been installed. "We have used 28 solar panels (each 12V, 70W) which have been used in two groups of 14 panels each," said Negi.

"Station building load has been segregated in two portions. Each portion is being fed by one group of solar panels. The complete work has been done departmentally by arranging solar panels from Kapurthala rail coach factory and solar charge controllers have been purchased from the market. All wiring, installation, commissioning has been done departmentally, without any outside assistance," he said

These measures of opting for renewable sources of energy, as explained above, can be easily replicated in the Indian military considering that they too operate in remote locations and face a similar dearth of energy, which most Indians have got used to. It is purely a matter of considering the alternative processes that are available to the leadership and then opting for one that (a) has the least environmental signature; (b) is easily adaptable;

and (c) is operationally suitable. The decision-making matrix of the military for optimising a process may be suitably modified to **focus on all the three mentioned variables**.

The juxtaposition of the present and future is very important in the making of an environmental leader. Presently, the environmental debate is fractured and the future is uncertain, to say the least. In such a scenario, it is only the bold within the military who will consider decision-making with environmental implications as a variable. The pragmatic approach would be to wait out the current controversy raging on the science of climate change and whether anthropogenic interventions have caused this state of affairs or not. But pragmatism in this case may be mirroring cynicism. Later may be too late. The timeframes of decisions may be allowed to be long when it is certain that the consequences of environment change may not be felt by us immediately. However, when sudden climatic events are affecting us with increasing and unpredictable regularity, it would be strategically important for a military leader to take these into account while planning operations. Another example of such prudence would be to consider the efforts that the militaries all over the world (including India) have to launch whenever a natural calamity strikes. To cater to such eventualities, both in terms of training and material, would be a leadership decision even though such requirements may not be directly imposed upon the military by the civil administration as a routine. The politics of disaster management is a separate subject in itself.

Over and above the strategy and benefits of environmental leadership mentioned here, the need to demonstrate environmental concerns in the military flows from their proclivity to showcase the institution of the military as an outstanding example of excellence in all walks of life. The citizens of the nation expect and would emulate this 'lead from the front' ethos of the military in this crucial facet of social entity. When the Indian government has designed the National Action Plan on Climate Change (NAPCC)[6] to prepare the country towards meeting its commitments in reducing greenhouse gas emissions, it would be a leadership decision on the part of the Indian military establishment to come forward with its own plan, within the ambit of the NAPCC, for the organisation, thus, helping the country meet this commitment. The state governments in India have formulated and implemented their own action plans on climate change. Although these policies are applicable to military installations in that state also, they are not required to provide a feedback on the implementation generally owing to the unique position that the military occupies in India.[7] This by no means absolves it from the responsibility of acting on the desired actions. It may prove to be a case of moral high ground for the military to be proactive and act on these action plans even when not specifically called upon to do so. Only by demonstrating this kind of leadership can it win the confidence and awe of the nation. Most of these plans have been so astutely designed that they are easily actionable and make economic sense too.

Impediments to Environmental Leadership in the Military

It may be a little difficult to understand that there may be impediments to the formulation and implementation of environmental policies in the Indian military, since it makes eminent sense – operationally, economically and socially – to do so. Why has this not gained acceptance in a big way, similar to the militaries of the developed nations? To answer this, it is important to understand the contemporary leadership value system and priorities that are followed in most of the military establishments around the globe and India is no exception.

The Indian military, as also the nation, is passing through a transition phase wherein it is modernising and formulating a strategy commensurate with the major and active role that the country is set to portray in the global affairs. The pace at which the transformation is taking place in the country's stature requires the military leadership to think 360^0, even while observing and imbibing the model followed by similarly placed military institutions. It has to charter a path with its own value system. Considering the geographical location of the country and its history, it is not surprising that uni-focus thinking on attaining military balance or superiority against its adversary is of utmost importance. This superiority is achieved primarily by means of numerical and technological dominance. The Indian military establishment is wholly involved in building, modernising and training for achieving these two objectives. It is still on the upward slope of the growth graph and is focussed primarily on improving its war-fighting abilities.

It has already been discussed earlier that the military establishments of developed nations (like the US, UK, etc) have now shifted their focus equally to their environmental responsibility. Their objective is not only to ensure an operationally efficient establishment but the path being chartered takes into account the changed realities of modern economics. They are open to deliberation of their actions having an impact on the environment. They now go past their personal value systems to observe the opportunity presented by following the low energy intensity as well as resource efficient and socially responsible path. Since 'environmental value' is comparatively a modern construct, the complexities associated with it have been appreciated early on by the countries that had a robust investment in scientific research. This is the underlying reason for the headstart that the developed countries have in the matter.

The policies on environmental management in different countries or communities are based on local interpretations of politics, economics, science, and culture, etc. This knowledge system is still evolving and is at different stages of consciousness in different countries. These complexities make it difficult for the military leadership in emerging power centres of the world to accept this as an important paradigm. For them, the orthodox martial outlook is the only necessity. For the sake of a better definition, this may be called a 'traditionalist approach' towards the fast evolving discourse of environment management within the military. It should not be construed that this approach is wrong; rather, it may be a necessity considering the state of affairs in many countries. The present-day asymmetry and complexities force the militaries to follow the rationalist approach to security. However, it is the belief of the author that the Indian military establishment, being one of the largest in the world, is rightly poised to show leadership on this front now. The business case made out previously in this chapter makes this vital for the Indian military establishment. The need is to rise above a set value system that has been handed down from one bureaucratic/military hierarchy to another, keeping the benefits of environmental leadership in abeyance.

It is not an easy task to plan for unknown timeframes as is the case in environmental matters. A logical military approach would normally not work when we are dealing with matters where the enemy is not known and even the attack timelines and place are also uncertain. Then it is easy to postpone a decision till clarity is built. The only argument against environmental forays, albeit weak, is that building process efficiency and thereby reducing costs does not need another strong driver for change. A military that has understood the concept of a lean and mean approach to operational readiness would embrace it openly. By going ahead on this path, a private enterprise might improve its balance sheet and since its prime responsibility is to its shareholders, it would earn kudos for the leadership demonstrated. A military organisation, on the other hand, does not have a profit motive. Therefore, if it adopts this leadership model, it would be akin to a private concern going beyond the regulatory requirements of following environmental bylaws. Why this happens is a separate study in itself.[8] This would normally happen either due to the top management's commitment or leadership on the subject or in a situation where the 'policy-supporters' manage to convince the 'non-believer' constituents of the long-term benefits and, thus, manage to tilt the leadership towards the subject. It is the advocacy of the problem and the solution – the quantum of change being a large factor, which ordinarily convinces the leadership to accept or reject the proposal for an activity that is not immediately required to be acted upon.

It must be clear by now that overcoming the impediments to showcase environmental leadership in the military is a task which would have to be driven by extrinsic variables as the uncertainties involved are too large for adoption by a hierarchy that has been largely inured to the traditional model of growth. The role model militaries (read those of the developed countries) are still studying further avenues to incorporate environmental forays. They have started realising the comprehensive benefits that this approach has accrued to them only now. Therefore, it would be worthwhile as it is not too late for the Indian military establishment to start thinking of formulating its own strategies of environmental leadership. Further chapters would showcase some of the avenues where and how the same can be incorporated.

Comparative Analysis…

A closer look at the advocacy of environmental leadership in our military, would suggest subtle drivers and impediments. While the drivers are both extrinsic and intrinsic, the impediments are purely intrinsic. It is the self-driven organisational belief and value system that has not yet ensured development of this format of leadership. Fig 1.1 would bring this argument in perspective.

Fig 1.1: Environmental Leadership in the Military

Drivers

- Economic sense
- Operational spin-offs
- Safe environment
- Socially responsible behaviour

Impediments

- Personal value system
- Priority set
- Perceived lack of need for following environmental leadership
- Uncertainty of results

The order of stating the drivers or the impediments is not necessarily commensurate with the importance attached to each. This order would vary with different individuals or organisations and is dependent upon the value system that they are used to. So there may be a case where the requirement to leave behind a safe environment may be the biggest motivator to adopt environmentally friendly practices. On the other hand, traditionalists may view the operational spin-off as the main achievement of following this path. In the same way, the impediments take priority, depending upon the individual's intrinsic thought process.

The need for environmental governance in the military cannot be overstated. It would suffice to say that the mindset of the higher military echelons to further the cause of the environment would now be counted as a strategic decision that would distinguish a modern military from one that is working towards it. The approach for adopting this paradigm would necessarily be innovative and customised for different military organisations. Various factors of input resources, geographical location, technological limitations and, above all, human will, would determine the approach that is finally undertaken whilst adopting an environmentally sound policy. The military leadership is looked up to in almost all countries. By adding another dimension to it, one that has social values and military ethos combined, the image of the military may see a positive transformation. Improving productivity within any business organisation is a priority of the top management and the military is in the same mould. This could be the first step to strive for by an environmental leader in the military.

Notes

1. For more information on the subject, readers may refer to Col P.K. Gautam (Retd) *Environmental Security: New Challenges and Role of Military* (New Delhi: Shipra Publications, 2010).
2. For more information on the subject, readers may refer to *Environment Change and National Security* by the author (New Delhi: KW Publishers, 2011).
3. This policy statement has been reproduced from the site www.sustainability.army.mil/overview/ArmyEnvStrategy.pdf, accessed on December 7, 2010.
4. http://www.environmentalleader.com/2009/04/28/military-adopts-green-technologies/, accessed on January 26, 2011.
5. Ibid.
6. http://pmindia.nic.in/climate_change.htm, accessed on February 2, 2011.
7. Readers may study the Delhi State Action Plan on Climate Change at http://moef.nic.in/downloads/public-information/Press_Delhi_NAP.pdf, accessed on February 3, 2011.
8. Readers may refer to Neil Gunningham, ed., *Corporate Environmental Responsibility* (US and England: Ashgate Publishing Limited, 2009); Aseem Prakash "Why do Firms Adopt 'Beyond-Compliance' Environmental Policies?" pp. 297-310.

2

Complexities of Waste Management in Air Force Installations

I think that our cities have the dubious distinction of being the dirtiest cities in the world. There is no doubt about it. But if there is a Nobel Prize for dirt and filth, India will win it hands down. There is no competition for that and we have to do something dramatic on municipal solid waste.

Indian Union Environment and
Forest Minister Jairam Ramesh[1]

There are many nuances associated with a safe environment but their relative appreciation is largely based on individual perceptions. When talking in terms of the military, the connotation of safety in matters of the environment is a foreign context due to a different priority set. In dealing with the issue, one has to constantly remind the reader that the environment here does not imply the 'security environment', rather the safety of our habitat from anthropogenic actions that are not martial in nature. Thus, while discussing the issue of waste management in military organisations, I have stayed clear of dealing with the subject of waste generated as a direct result of military acts of war and the controversial subject of nuclear waste (especially in the aftermath of the nuclear accident in Japan *circa* March 2011 tsunami).

Waste primarily falls into two categories: hazardous and non-hazardous. Both include a wide variety of materials, but generally, hazardous waste falls under stricter regulations and covers a range of chemicals and other wastes. Non-hazardous waste is known as Municipal Solid Waste (MSW) and is what is commonly known as garbage, including household waste. Generally a sub-category of hazardous waste known as Industrial Solid Waste (ISW), has long been the single biggest source of waste generated globally. Every manufacturing and hardware maintenance process produces waste but the biggest generators include chemical, paper and food manufacturers, utilities, leather, plastic, metals manufacturers, textile manufacturers, petroleum companies, and machinery manufacturers. Since a military base uses many of these maintenance and manufacturing processes while supporting military training, ISW is a normal byproduct.

This chapter would deal with a case study on management of waste generated as a result of day-to-day activities in Air Force formations. The waste generated therein is of the two genres described above i.e. MSW and ISW. The methodology used for their respective treatment cannot be seamlessly clubbed together as their generation and disposal processes are different to a large extent. MSW is generated in both domestic and technical areas. Domestic areas are those where the Service personnel and their families reside while the technical areas are those where flying and ground-based training along with support activities like maintenance of military hardware and communication systems, estate administration, etc., are routinely carried out. By virtue of the fact that personnel operate in these areas, MSW is likely to be generated there too. The disposal of MSW from these clearly demarcated parts of the Air Force formation (domestic and technical) is, however, common.

On the other hand ISW (including purely liquid industrial waste) is generated from within the operational area of the formation. Whenever the preventive maintenance activities of military hardware are carried out, it would generate ISW. It would include (amongst many others):

- Rags for cleaning.
- Hazardous waste like used mineral oils, greases, fuel, hydraulic oils, etc.
- Consumable metallic, rubberised and plastic miscellaneous parts.
- Packaging for spares, tools, FOL (Fuel, Oil and Lubricant), and consumable parts.

Their disposal would obviously involve a different procedure as these are toxic in nature due to the presence of metallic particles and inorganic chemicals and are, thus, categorised under hazardous waste. Most of these are non-biodegradable and again demand a different way of handling.

Why Manage Waste?

When the military has so many different variables to manage, the mundane subject of 'waste management' hardly seems to be a subject worthy of consideration in the overall context of environmental leadership. This thought process needs to be suitably moulded by considering waste management as a resource efficiency initiative. The world today talks of the 'cradle-to-cradle' approach as different from the 'cradle-to-grave' designs of products. It has been realised that resources that are allowed to become waste as in cradle to grave designs, add to our overall costs and inefficiency. Not only do we then need to add value to raw material to produce afresh, we also need to create support processes for sustaining the product chain. On the other hand, if the product value is maintained by change of environs, partial build-up or reusing the important and valuable ingredient, it results in a cradle to cradle approach. Then it gives rise to resource efficiency.

The need for building resource efficiency necessitates following the principle of the three 'Rs' – Reduce, Reuse, and Recycle – while dealing with waste management and product use. While these may not always satisfy the rigours associated with military equipment, there is no denying that an audit of various processes that are undertaken in support of IAF operations, in this context, can lead to reduced generation of waste, therefore, reduced demands for replacement and, finally, overall cost reduction.

There are apparent purely environmental safety forays when we deal with management of MSW. However, there are good practices that need to be followed even in this venture, not only for the environmental benefits (and the associated paybacks) but also for improving the quality of life of the inhabitants of the formation, the flight safety of operating aircraft and for generating a feel of positive energy about the formation. All these issues come to the fore when MSW is effectively managed by ensuring cleanliness of the formation. I have specifically alluded to positive energy when talking in terms of a military formation. This is because most of these formations are small townships in their own right, with a set pattern of lifestyle, distinctive from the adjoining civilian community.

What differentiates a military cluster is the impression of orderliness as one enters the gates of a formation, which is normally a little removed from the city or town. If the same is allowed to deteriorate to a standard wherein the military personnel or their families stop taking pride in their surroundings, it would become difficult for the formation commander and the personnel that he/she commands to be able to focus completely on the critical tasks at hand, dealing with complex machines, explosives and other life threatening processes, on a day-to-day basis. This is because presently there are so many other distractions that a military person and his/her family are exposed to, and the cord that connects them to the military style of living is the pride that they have in their profession, and the military formation is representative of the same.

As already mentioned earlier, not only the requirement to showcase the military leadership on aspects related to community living but also environmental concerns dictate the requirement to manage waste in military formations. Similar concerns have prompted the Indian government to legislate on the subject. These rules and regulations are equally relevant to any military formation. A summary of these is placed below in the Table 2.1.

Table 2.1 Legislations and Relevant Agencies Related to Waste Management in India

Related Legislation	Enforcement Agencies
Article 21 of the Constitution	Maintenance of health and preservation of sanitation primarily fall under the purview of this Article of the Constitution. There are other Articles (on health, etc.) which cover the subject.
The Municipal Solid Wastes (Management and Handling) Rules, 2000	It has defined 'municipal solid waste' as 'commercial and residential wastes generated in a municipal or notified areas in either solid or semi-solid form *excluding* industrial hazardous wastes, but including treated bio-medical wastes.'[2]

Hazardous Wastes (Management and Handling) Amendment Rules, 2003	These rules classify used mineral oil as hazardous waste under the Hazardous Waste (Management and Handling) Rules, 2003, that requires proper handling and disposal. The organisation will seek authorisation for disposal of hazardous waste from the concerned State Pollution Control Boards (SPCB) as and when required.[3]

To understand the seriousness attached to the subject and to add a glossary of terminology used in the context of waste management, relevant provisions of the '**The Municipal Solid Wastes (Management and Handling) Rules,** 2000' are placed at Appendix 'A'. These rules highlight the work that needs to be carried out for managing waste in any community. An IAF formation is in itself a small community that works actively on this front. Even though the rules may not apply directly to all IAF formations, their relevance as guidelines in managing waste in the formations cannot be denied. It is on the ways to improve the system further that the present case study on this environmentally relevant subject is being undertaken.

Case Study Methodology

Once it is clear that waste management in the IAF relates not merely to effective garbage disposal but is a palimpsest of resource efficiency, it becomes more 'respectful' to talk of this mundane issue. How should the subject be treated is the next question that needs to be tackled. The subject would be dealt as a case study of two IAF formations that are operationally very different and have been chosen as a representative sample from where extrapolation can be done to undertake a rough inventory of waste generation in the IAF, good practices being followed/can be followed and, finally, make some recommendations that can be incorporated after customisation. A questionnaire was forwarded to these formations for collating the details of waste management processes being followed there. This questionnaire is attached at Appendix 'B' to the chapter. It would be prudent to explain the rationale behind the design of the questionnaire and expected outcome of the case study.

Data Collection and Analysis

The first step is obviously to understand the quantum and types of waste generated and, thus, the task at hand, for undertaking their safe disposal. This would also involve studying the scope and avenues for implementing the good practices concerned with waste disposal. This research component includes, but is not limited to, the following tasks:

- Collect and review data. Analysis of the data to be discussed with the concerned staff within the organisation and other responsible agencies.
- Review and analyse previous relevant reports, data (if available) and related information, including lessons learned from the past. If these are not available, then suggest ways to generate and maintain such data in the future.
- Review the technologies/methodologies currently employed for disposal or the Municipal and Industrial Waste Management System (M&IWMS) and assess their impact on the environment.
- Review the organisational framework under which the task is being performed within the formation. Analyse the information, determine the impact of the present levels of service, and recommend the required service levels for various conditions [including residential, commercial (unit run ventures), and industrial areas (for maintenance intensive operations)].
- Recommend changes and improvements – taking into consideration development trends.
- Study the requirement of increase in service levels and how adequate they would be for meeting the enhanced disposal task.
- Generally, place the sample of the case study in perspective. Recommend establishing a monitoring programme that can be implemented in the long run as a follow-up to the study carried out herein.

This research project is being undertaken to serve as a guideline for the higher military echelons to decide upon the best course of action available to them for management of waste in the military formations. The study is equally useful for a medium sized industrial community in the civil space. Since each military formation is unique, designing a 'fit all' SOP (Standard

Operating Procedure) is not feasible with the present level of study. This study will help in developing only strategic plans to guide the formation's waste management plan.

Existing Realities: The Study

Treatment of MSW is quite different from the way industrial waste is disposed of in the IAF. One of the major differences is that disposal of MSW is normally outsourced through a conservancy contract as the local governmental bodies cannot provide the requisite support owing to the location of the Air Force installations. On the other hand, industrial waste consisting of chemical sludge and waste oils, etc. is treated in-house, in the predominantly maintenance set-up of the IAF, before disposal. As a practice, the waste mineral oils are normally returned to the Army Supply Corps (ASC) units for central disposal at their end. Chemicals used for industrial processes like electroplating and degreasing are treated in-house before being released in the drainage. In this context, while explaining the findings of the study, it would be prudent to cover it under two different sections, as per the type of the waste being dealt with.

Municipal Waste

As already mentioned above, the methodology for MSW disposal was found to be similar between the two different formations of the IAF, with concessions for local peculiarities. However, there was a need for standardisation of important and environmentally sensitive clauses in the MSW disposal outsourcing conservancy tender notice as well as its contract. The major findings with regards to municipal waste are listed below.

- The general awareness level of the families towards cleanliness and safe disposal of both biodegradable and non-biodegradable types of MSW was found to be very good. As expected, they took pride in how their surroundings were being maintained. Even a slight deterioration in the standards was a cause for consternation. Therefore, the focus of the administration towards this issue is rightly justified for social reasons too.

- For controlling the bird menace in and around Air Force formations (birds are attracted to municipal waste and their collision with aircraft can/does cause major catastrophes) and, thus, enhancing the flight safety. The Director General (Inspection and Safety) branch of the IAF has issued instructions for safe disposal of the waste. The administrations were found receptive and concerned towards this aspect of waste disposal, too.
- The two major formations observed for this study had a population of around 5,000 although their operations varied considerably.
- The conservancy contract for disposal of MSW was entered into after floating comprehensively documented tenders. These generally specified the place where the MSW was to be collected from and disposed of. The disposal site was supposed to be at a minimum distance from the station and had to be a local municipality cleared site. However, this was an observed weak area. More on this issue would be covered when the standardisation of the tender and contract are dealt with.
- Waste collection was being done door-to-door as also from the bins constructed in the domestic area. In the operations/technical area, waste collection was from the bins only, where there was no segregation at source. To be fair, unlike in the domestic area, the waste generated in the operations area was mostly food waste and, thus, there was no great need for segregation at source. In the domestic area, the segregation (biodegradable/non-biodegradable) was being done by the conservancy contractor labourers. However, this was not observed to be a standard practice and needs immediate correction.
- The collection was being done by carts and/or motorised vehicles and then transported to the disposal site in motorised vehicles. The vehicles were not closed in all the cases, though this was specified in the contract and also a legal requirement.
- There was no data available as to the amount of waste collected and disposed of by the contractor. At present, there is no requirement to maintain this data even for statistical purposes by the formation.
- The formations were still deliberating upon local level vermiculture initiatives that some stations in the IAF have initiated. Lack of clarity on

the methodology to be adopted as well as the economics involved in the process of setting up this venture was resulting in it not taking off even though some formations had initiated the process. At one formation, there was no need for vermin-composting due to negligible demand for the final product, the soil being so fertile. The formation was yet to decide on the future of the initiative undertaken.

- The iron waste basket provided as part of the furniture in government accommodation was of no practical use for various reasons. Due to lack of proper provisioning and, to a great extent, lack of knowledge, it was not feasible for the households to separate the waste in two separate receptacles before handing it over to the conservancy labourers.
- The conservancy contract rates had shown a high upswing when the door-to-door collection was introduced due to operational and environmental considerations.
- The methodology for ensuring the requisite services from the conservancy contractor was not elaborately spelt out.

Industrial Waste

There were many sources of generation of industrial waste in an IAF formation. Obviously, in a predominantly overhaul and maintenance formation, the industrial waste generated was far greater than in a typical flying formation. The treatment of the waste was also differently tackled. These sources of generation of waste in an IAF formation and the major findings are listed below.

- Degreasing and electroplating baths.
- Ultrasonic filter cleaning baths.
- Waste Aviation Turbine Fuel (ATF) and aviation oils/lubes
- Waste Mechanical Transport (MT) oil and lubes
- E-waste – old computers, etc.
- Packing materials.

- The degreasing and electroplating baths were connected to the treatment plant before the discharge was allowed to flow into the sewers. The pH value of the discharge was monitored every day after its treatment was carried out. This process has been sanctioned vide an Air Force publication. However, the treatment plants now being put in operation go beyond the stipulations of the publication and are superior in ensuring the treatment of waste before disposal.

- The waste mineral oil from the ultrasonic filter cleaning baths was not disposed of as per the general regulations. Specific instructions for its disposal were not available.
- Waste ATF was being disposed of in a very transparent manner by reusing it as cleaning material. Whatever waste MT lubes and oils were being returned, were being disposed of in a fairly methodological manner by returning them to ASC. These were being disposed of as per the stipulations of the logistics procedures given in the relevant Air Force publication.
- There was no requirement to measure the waste mineral oils being returned vis-à-vis the oil issued; the quantity being returned was accepted with no focus on the timeframe and type of oil. Thus, there were instances in which a particular waste lube was not returned for a couple of years altogether even though the issue/usage was going on during that period. Therefore, it was not possible to judge the losses due to spillage or transportation that could be used as benchmark figures to confirm the veracity of the quantity being returned. It was difficult to generate statistics on the amount of waste being returned as a percentage of total non-consumable mineral lubes (MT oils, aviation hydraulic oil, etc.) being issued due to a large mismatch of data. However, it could be safely assumed that less than 30 percent of such waste oils were being recovered and disposed of safely.
- There were no guidelines on reuse of packing material received with equipment being purchased or received from depots; it was left to local initiative which was found to be good in a few instances.
- Guidelines/instructions on disposal of e-waste have been issued by the service and regional Headquarters (HQ). The database of vendors dealing with e-waste disposal was made available through these instructions.
- The lead recovered from firing of small arms ammunition in the ground firing ranges[4] at Air Force formations was not being returned by the armament section in all cases. In the stations that were following this

practice, the recovery was being done manually after every firing and during periodic maintenance when sieving was being done. This lead was then being disposed of centrally through the Metal Scrap Trading Corporation (MSTC) Ltd[5]. The formations were not aware of the retrieval methodology, timeframes and even the requirement to do so. Similarly, there was no cross-check of the issue, and if the armament section failed to return the lead being retrieved or did not retrieve the same, there was no feedback process. The publication on the subject was of very old vintage and vague.

The Path Untrod

The findings listed above are broad-based and a few formations in the IAF could be doing much more on these issues. However, standardisation of good practices on this front is of the essence here. These good practices can be adopted by any military formation as well as civilian community. Based on the above, there are a few important issues that merit focus and could be in the form of an organisation-wide order. These issues are listed below.

- Standardisation of important clauses of the conservancy tender and contract dealing with disposal of MSW.
- Systemic changes to ensure compliance with MSW disposal rules, 2000.
- Specific guidelines on disposal of waste oil and lubes.
- Instructions on waste metal.
- Waste reuse instructions.

Since these instructions would cover a broad canvas, the endeavour here would be to tag the salient issues that can be then expanded and customised by any organisation to suit its specific context.

Contours of the First Steps

- **MSW Management and Disposal Contracts:** Since conservancy contracts are being entered into by all military formations, they should incorporate standard environmentally mandatory features. The features given in the tender document and the contract would be almost on the same lines due to the legalities involved. The formal requirements to be incorporated in a Request For Proposal (RFP) are specified in the defence manuals and, hence, these are not being repeated here. The proposed standard features given below are focussed on good environmental practices only. These should not be construed as limiting the scope of the tender or contract:

- **Contract Period:** This is obviously a legal requirement and has to be so stated upfront.
- **Definition of Waste:**
  - What exactly is the waste that needs to be disposed of? The formation should include foliage, food and other household wastes as part of the contract.
  - Normally, the waste that goes through the sewers does not form a part of the conservancy contract.
  - While defining waste, it would be a good practice to bifurcate it under biodegradable and non-biodegradable waste. This would help in enforcing segregation at source, which is the norm as per the good practices of waste management. Thus, this has to be made a mandatory requirement of the contract.
- **Geographical Limits of Collection:**
  - The first and foremost feature of the two documents would be to define the areas that require conservancy support. This should mandatorily mention door-to-door collection of segregated waste.
  - For the contractor to understand the quantum of work involved for quoting realistic rates, it would be prudent to mention the number of households at each location and the messes that would need the support.
  - The number of bins at each location that are required to be emptied (mostly for foliage and for maintaining common area cleanliness) should also be mentioned clearly.
- **Mode and Methodology of Collection:**
  - It is a requirement as per the municipal waste rules that the door-to-door waste collection should be by manual means and preferably

not by vehicles running on fossil fuels, for obvious reasons. Thereafter, the disposal of waste to the actual site or landfill may be by vehicles that have to be sufficiently enclosed from the sides. Use of tractor trolleys or open tempos should not be permitted.

- Segregation of waste has to be made mandatory for the labour. For this, it has to be made essential that the collection carts and vehicles should have separate receptacles for ensuring their segregation.
- The practice of specifying and limiting the number of labourers required to complete the task is not right. With the quantum of work specified correctly, it should be left to the contractor to complete the task to the satisfaction of the authorities at the military formation.

- **Periodicity and Timing of Collection:**
  - The periodicity of collection and timings of the visit of the conservancy labourers at each site of collection has to be pre-specified.
  - This also needs wide communication to the community being serviced as overflowing waste bins are not a healthy sight. The security aspects of civil labour entering restricted areas are, thus, catered for.
- **Disposal Location:**
  - The disposal location of the municipal waste can be a landfill/ suitable site authorised by the local municipality. Merely specifying the minimum distance from the formation where the waste is to be disposed of is not sufficient.
  - Onus of safe disposal of waste still vests with the formation authorities.
  - If within the formation, the waste is being utilised for vermi-composting, then that also needs to be specified in the tender documents and contract as it directly affects the workload and economics of the conservancy operation. To make the project economical, even sharing of day-to-day compositing costs and produce between the contractor and the Air Force formation can be thought of.

- **Ensuring Performance:**
  - To ensure continued performance from the contractor, a performance guarantee amount should be sought as part of the contract. This guarantee should be invoked in case poor quality of service is seen during the contract period. Adequate legal safeguards need to be inbuilt into the contract for this purpose. It may also include blacklisting of the contractor in case of deficiency of services.
  - Specifying the number of labourers who should perform the task may not guarantee the services of requisite standards. Specifying the exact services required, coupled with a performance guarantee, may be a better solution for ensuring the same.

Box 1

Systemic Changes in Handling of Municipal Waste

While the personnel of a military formation and their families aspire for a greener and cleaner environment, their knowledge of their contribution (adverse or otherwise) to the same is limited. The organisation also does not really ensure that they do their bit by capacity building or provision of infrastructure that would ensure good practices being followed as a default.

Waste segregation at source is a desirable feature of any waste disposal system. It would then be prudent to provide two waste bins of different colours for each household wherein they can segregate the biodegradable and non-biodegradable waste and hand over the same to the conservancy labourer. These bins should form part of the normal scale of furniture authorised to military personnel. Of course, what waste constitutes a part of which of the two bins, would have to be explained through capacity building exercises undertaken at the formation level. This would also help the conservancy labour speed up their work.

Most of the non-biodegradable products can be sold by the conservancy contractor (the waste being his property) to recyclers, thus, generating funds for him. This can be leveraged by the military formation to seek lower rates of waste disposal from the conservancy contractor.

It would also ensure that at no stage can the military formation or community be held responsible of dumping the non-biodegradable waste in municipal landfills, which is prohibited under law.

- **Industrial Waste Management:** Waste mineral oils are also categorised as hazardous waste. Their management is of utmost importance for securing the health of the troops and their families. The main weaknesses in the present system that have been noticed are (a) lack of awareness of the consequences of action; (b) absence of instructions necessitating collection of waste oils; and (c) waste reuse is almost non-existent, again, due to lack of awareness. To overcome these weaknesses, an organisation-wide awareness of good practices proposed below would be required.
    - **Inventory Mapping:**
        - The plan for safe disposal can commence only after drawing up an inventory of oils and lubes that are not fully consumed during the operation of the hardware. This exercise would have to be performed across different cells/departments/directorates at the Service HQ that oversee maintenance operations relating to MT and other weapon platforms.
        - Even for oils and lubes that are partially consumed before periodic flushing, a rate of return can be laid down by the Service HQ. This would have to be done in consultation with the field formations.
    - **Documentation:**
        - At present, all the waste oils are treated under one nomenclature reference, thus, making it almost impossible to correlate the type of waste oil being returned (or not being returned). This process would have to be modified suitably so as to be able to provide a feedback to the maintenance and logistics military personnel on the need to take specific controlling steps.
        - The next step would be to issue instructions to all field formations for correlating issues of the non-consumable oils vis-a-vis returns of their waste on a quarterly/monthly basis. With computerisation of the inventory, issue and receipt procedures, this process should not take much time. The correlation should be done for a few months on a trial basis to generate data on the ratio of oil that is recoverable. With these benchmark figures

then available, instructions on handling of the waste oil should be issued that would be applicable for the entire organisation.

- The final disposal of waste oil would continue to be through ASC, as is being done. The quantity of waste oil returned should show a significant increase if the documentation is changed as per the proposal given above.

- **Metal Waste:** The metal waste is mostly accounted for and properly disposed of in the IAF due to the costs involved. The process is well audited. Still, there are areas that demand some caution. One of these is listed below.
  - There are no specific instructions on retrieving lead fired at the small arms range in each Air Force formation. The ill effect of not doing so has already been covered earlier. It is recommended to retrieve this lead normally, on a daily basis after the firing. Thereafter, on a quarterly (or bi-annually) basis, at the time of range butt maintenance by the Military Engineering Services (MES) (or its counterpart), sifting of the butt filling should be done by the use of wired meshes and the lead should be retrieved. The retrieved lead has to be returned for disposal through MSTC. The responsibility of this retrieval would rest with the concerned stakeholders dealing with armament stores. These orders need to be formalised for each and every IAF formation.

Capacity Building

Regular capacity building lectures on the subject of waste management for a healthy environment may be planned by the medical and maintenance staff at field and regional HQ levels. Inviting experts on the subject from the civil field should also be encouraged. This issue would be covered in detail, in the subsequent chapter on Environmental Training.

Box 2
Waste Reuse

Some of the air-dropped armament stores in the IAF are transported in wooden crates/boxes. Due to the weight of the stores, these crates/boxes break during transportation. The wood is changed and the crates/boxes repaired. The broken wood is returned to stores under the waste wood nomenclature and then sold off as such.

In the small arms range in any Air Force formation, the arms are fired on paper targets that are glued onto wooden frames. These wooden frames are made in the local workshop. Wood for manufacturing these frames is purchased from the local market. During firing, these frames are almost fully destroyed as splinters.

If some portion of the waste wood generated from the broken boxes is usable and can be converted to usable wood nomenclature by undertaking suitable documentation, then this wood can be issued to the workshop and the wooden frames can be manufactured out of it. This would not only save money but also ensure less usage of wood, which in itself is a good environmental practice.

Such examples of waste reuse are plenty in the IAF. There is a need to learn from each other through regular exchange of ideas at various levels of the hierarchy. Only then can an organisation-wide environmental leadership culture prevail.

Complexities Unravelled

While dealing with issues of waste management in defence installations, it is imperative to have the right perspective. The priority of a defence organisation is always going to be operational preparedness, and rightly so. However, that should not deter a military commander from following the appropriate path for disposal of waste – correctly and judiciously.

The path for safe waste disposal is already well documented in the IAF. The strategic planners of yore have done due justice to the process, be it municipal waste or industrial. It is now required to contemporise it so that a focussed approach to the subject leads to visible gains. Whether it is done by issue of organisation-wide instructions or by amendment to the existing publications, is left to the Service HQ to decide. The focus should be to ensure that the process of safe disposal is standardised and then crosschecked by the inspecting teams. In kick-starting this process, it is also important to first lay down realistic benchmark figures that can be adhered to. It is definitely not envisaged that this system would lead to more paper work at any level. For the process to succeed, capacity building of all personnel would be very important. Capacity building can be carried out at the field as well as regional HQ level.

The methodology adopted for undertaking this study had a few weaknesses. Most glaring amongst them was the small sample size. However, what was lacking by way of limited scope of research was made up to some extent by discussing this issue with many experienced stakeholders. That the issue is required to be given more focus, was the common thread noticed during the course of this study.

Appendix 'A'[6]

Ministry of Environment and Forests
Notification
New Delhi, the 25th September, 2000

1. **Short title and commencement:**
   1. These rules may be called the Municipal Solid Wastes (Management and Handling) Rules, 2000.
   2. Save as otherwise provided in these rules, they shall come into force on the date of their publication in the Official Gazette.
2. **Application:** These rules shall apply to every municipal authority responsible for collection, segregation, storage, transportation,, processing and disposal of municipal solid wastes.
3. **Definitions:** In these rules, unless the context otherwise requires,
   i. "**anaerobic digestion**" means a controlled process involving microbial decomposition of organic matter in the absence of oxygen;
   ii. "**authorisation**" means the consent given by the Board or Committee to the "operator of a facility" ;
   iii. "**biodegradable substance**" means a substance that can be degraded by micro-organisms;

iv. **"biomethanation"** means a process which entails enzymatic decomposition of the organic matter by microbial action to produce methane rich biogas;

v. "**collection**" means lifting and removal of solid wastes from collection points or any other location;

vi. "**composting**" means a controlled process involving microbial decomposition of organic matter;

vii. "**demolition and construction waste**" means wastes from building materials debris and rubble resulting from construction, remodelling, repair and demolition operation;

viii. "**disposal**" means final disposal of municipal solid wastes in terms of the specified measures to prevent contamination of ground water, surface water and ambient air quality;

ix. **"form"** means a form appended to these rules;

x. **"generator of wastes"** means persons or establishments generating municipal solid wastes;

xi. "**landfilling**" means disposal of residual solid wastes on land in a facility designed with protective measures against pollution of ground water, surface water and air fugitive dust, wind-blown litter, bad odour, fire hazard, bird menace, pests or rodents, greenhouse gas emissions, slope instability and erosion;

xii. "**leachate**" means liquid that seeps through solid wastes or other medium and has extracts of dissolved or suspended material from it;

xiii. "**lysimeter**" is a device used to measure the rate of movement of water through or from a soil layer or is used to collect percolated water for quality analysis;

xiv. **"municipal authority"** means Municipal Corporation, Municipality, Nagar Palika, Nagar Nigam, Nagar Panchayat, Municipal Council including a Notified Area Committee (NAC) or any other local body constituted under the relevant statutes and, where the management and handling of municipal solid waste is entrusted to such agency;

xv. **"municipal solid waste"** includes commercial and residential wastes generated in a municipal or notified area in either solid or semi-solid form, excluding industrial hazardous wastes but including treated bio-medical wastes;

xvi. **"operator of a facility"** means a person who owns or operates a facility for collection, segregation, storage, transportation, processing and disposal of municipal solid wastes and also includes any other agency appointed as such by the municipal authority for the management and handling of municipal solid wastes in the respective areas;

xvii. **"pelletisation"** means a process whereby pellets are prepared which are small cubes or cylindrical pieces made out of solid wastes, and includes fuel pellets which are also referred to as refuse derived fuel;

xviii. "**processing"** means the process by which solid wastes are transformed into new or recycled products;

xix. "**recycling"** means the process of transforming segregated solid wastes into raw materials for producing new products, which may or may not be similar to the original products;

xx. **"schedule"** means a schedule appended to these rules;

xxi. **"segregation"** means to separate the municipal solid wastes into the groups of organic, inorganic, recyclables and hazardous wastes;

xxii. **"State Board or the Committee"** means the State Pollution Control Board of a state, or as the case may be, the Pollution Control Committee of a union territory;

xxiii. **"storage"** means the temporary containment of municipal solid wastes in a manner so as to prevent littering, attraction to vectors, stray animals and excessive foul odour;

xxiv. **"transportation"** means conveyance of municipal solid wastes from place to place hygienically through a specially designed transport system so as to prevent foul odour, littering, unsightly conditions and accessibility to vectors;

xxv. "**vadose water"** water which occurs between the ground, surface and the water table that is the unsaturated zone;

xxvi. "**vermicomposting"** is a process of using earthworms for conversion of bio-degradable wastes into compost.

4. **Responsibility of municipal authority:**
   1. Every municipal authority shall, within the territorial area of the municipality, be responsible for the implementation of the provisions of these rules, and for any infrastructure development for collection, storage, segregation, transportation, processing and disposal of municipal solid wastes.
   2. The municipal authority or an operator of a facility shall make an application in **Form-I,** for grant of authorisation for setting up waste processing and disposal facility, including landfills from the State Board or Committee in order to comply with the implementation programme laid down in **Schedule I**.
   3. The municipal authority shall comply with these rules as per the implementation schedule laid down in **Schedule I.**

Schedule -II
[see rules 6(1) and (3), 7(1)]
Management of Municipal Solid Wastes

S. no.	Parameters	Compliance Criteria
1.	**Collection of municipal solid wastes**	1. Littering of municipal solid waste shall be prohibited in cities, towns and in urban areas notified by the State Governments. To prohibit littering and facilitate compliance, the following steps shall be taken by the municipal authority, namely: i. Organising house-to-house collection of municipal solid wastes through any of the methods, like community bin collection (central bin), house-to-house collection, collection on regular pre-informed timings and scheduling by using bell ringing of musical vehicle (without exceeding permissible noise levels); ii. Devising collection of waste from slums and squatter areas or localities, including hotels, restaurants, office complexes and commercial areas;

		iii. Wastes from slaughter houses, meat and fish markets, fruits and vegetable markets, which are biodegradable in nature, shall be managed to make use of such wastes; iv Bio-medical wastes and industrial wastes shall not be mixed with municipal solid wastes and such wastes shall follow the rules separately specified for the purpose; v. Collected waste from residential and other areas shall be transferred to the community bin by hand-driven containerised carts or other small vehicles; vi. Horticlutural and construction or demolition wastes or debris shall be separately collected and disposed of following proper norms. Similarly, wastes generated at dairies shall be regulated in accordance with the state laws; vii. Waste (garbage, dry leaves) shall not be burnt; viii. Stray animals shall not be allowed to move around waste storage facilities or at any other place in the city or town and shall be managed in accordance with the state laws. 2. The municipal authority shall notify the waste collection schedule and the likely method to be adopted, for public benefit, in a city or town. 3. It shall be the responsibility of the generator of wastes to avoid littering and ensure delivery of wastes in accordance with the collection and segregation system to be notified by the municipal authority as per para 1(2) of this Schedule.
2.	**Segregation of municipal solid wastes**	In order to encourage the citizens, the municipal authority shall organise awareness programmes for segregation of wastes and shall promote recycling or reuse of segregated materials. The municipal authority shall undertake a phased programme to ensure community participation in waste segregation. For this purpose, regular meetings at quarterly intervals shall be arranged by the municipal authorities with representatives of local resident welfare associations and non-governmental organisations.

3.	**Storage of municipal solid wastes**	Municipal authorities shall establish and maintain storage facilities in such a manner that they do not create unhygienic and unsanitary conditions around it. The following criteria shall be taken into account while establishing and maintaining storage facilities, namely: i. Storage facilities shall be created and established by taking into account quantities of waste generation in a given area and the population densities. A storage facility shall be so placed that it is accessible to users; ii. Storage facilities to be set up by municipal authorities or any other agency shall be so designed that wastes stored are not exposed to open atmosphere and shall be aesthetically acceptable and user-friendly; iii. Storage facilities or bins shall have easy to operate design for handling, transfer and transportation of waste. Bins for storage of biodegradable wastes shall be painted green, those for storage of recyclable wastes shall be printed white and those for storage of other wastes shall be printed black; iv Manual handling of waste shall be prohibited. If unavoidable due to constraints, manual handling shall be carried out under proper precaution with due care for the safety of workers.
4.	**Transportation of municipal solid wastes**	Vehicles used for transportation of wastes shall be covered. Waste should not be visible to the public, nor exposed to the open environment, preventing its scattering. The following criteria shall be met, namely: i. The storage facilities set up by municipal authorities shall be daily attended for clearing of wastes. The bins or containers wherever placed shall be cleaned before they start overflowing; ii. Transportation vehicles shall be so designed that multiple handling of wastes, prior to final disposal, is avoided.

5.	**Processing of municipal solid wastes**	Municipal authorities shall adopt suitable technology or combination of such technologies to make use of wastes so as to minimise burden on landfill. The following criteria shall be adopted, namely: i. The biodegradable wastes shall be processed by composting, vermicomposting, anaerobic digestion or any other appropriate biological processing for stabilisation of wastes. It shall be ensured that compost or any other end product shall comply with standards as specified in Schedule-IV; ii. Mixed waste containing recoverable resources shall follow the route of recycling. Incineration with or without energy recovery including pelletisation can also be used for processing wastes in specific cases. The municipal authority or the operator of a facility wishing to use other state-of-the-art technologies shall approach the Central Pollution Control Board to get the standards laid down before applying for grant of authorisation.
6.	**Disposal of municipal solid wastes**	Land filling shall be restricted to non-biodegradable, inert waste and other waste that is not suitable either for recycling or for biological processing. Land filling shall also be carried out for residues of waste processing facilities as well as pre-processing rejects from waste processing facilities. Land filling of mixed waste shall be avoided unless the same is found unsuitable for waste processing. Under unavoidable circumstances or till installation of alternate facilities, land-filling shall be done following proper norms. Landfill sites shall meet the specifications as given in Schedule III.

Appendix 'B'

Waste Management System in Air Force (AF) Stations

The questionnaire has been prepared to study the Municipal and Industrial Waste Management System (M&IWMS) being adopted in representative Air Force Stations. The information sought is open source.

The information contained herein would be utilised as a representative sample information of the IAF and is not reflective of any particular formation.

Please provide information to the following questions:

General Information

1. Name of the wing/station:
2. Area covered by the station:
3. Number of personnel in the station including families:
4. Number of messes/cafeterias (please specify types and strength):

Waste Disposal System

5. Method of disposal of Municipal Solid Waste (MSW): Incinerator/Landfill/Any other (specify)
6. Number of waste disposal/collection sites in the station:
7. Please attach document inviting conservancy contract bid (where feasible) of the previous year:
8. Is segregation of recyclable/non-recyclable waste done at source/any other point and how:
9. Is the data on amount of MSW and industrial waste generated in the previous year, available: Yes/No (If yes, please specify the qty)
10. Types of industrial waste generated and their disposal system (separately) being followed (industrial waste could be used cleaning material waste, used FOL, old packing material, etc):
11. Does the station have a policy on reducing/reusing/recycling (3Rs) the waste generation (MSW and industrial). Please attach the policy/or give a small summary:
12. Any visible effect/result of 3Rs policy:
13. Mode of collection of MSW:
14. Any waste exchange programme being carried out, then between which sections/units (please give details):
15. Total amount spent on conservancy of MSW and industrial waste, annually.

Notes

1. http://news.in.msn.com/national/article.aspx?cp-documentid=3432316, accessed on March 24, 2011. The minister made this statement in November 2009.
2. http://www.nlsenlaw.org/waste-management/articles/solid-waste-management2014an-indian-legal-profile/, accessed on March 24, 2011. The Indian judiciary system has been proactively tasking the municipal utilities to effectively do their duty towards waste management. For more on the subject readers, may wish to refer to this site.
3. http://sjvn.nic.in/projects/environmental-regulations.pdf, accessed on March 24, 2011
4. For more on the subject, please refer to Chapter 3, wherein a case study on armament training has been discussed.
5. For more information on MSTC Ltd (a Government of India enterprise) please visit http://www.mstcindia.co.in/. Their punch line is "Generate Wealth from Waste."
6. http://envfor.nic.in/legis/hsm/mswmhr.html, accessed on March 25, 2011. These are extracts of the legislation. Readers may wish to access the site for complete Act.

3

Building Resource Efficiency: Case Study – Armaments

Environment and Material Parsimony

The application of human intellect has led to many innovations. Knowingly or unknowingly, these innovations have had a tremendous impact on life on this planet. From the advent of the wheel to the journeys in space, human quest for "development" is exciting and equally frightening. It is frightening, because of the innovations that have brought the human race to a point of no return. The invention of dynamite and atomic devices falls in this category. Does this mean that innovations are anathema for mankind? Far from it, innovations are an integral part of the evolutionary process. It is the methodology involved in our development that demands introspection.

Nature has been accommodating and innovating to keep abreast of the rapid deterioration brought about by unsustainable consumption of natural resources. The beauty of innovation on the part of nature is that it is doing so by using and reusing mostly the same set of elements that it began with – namely, carbon, hydrogen and oxygen. It does not allow these elements to be wasted and reuses them in some form or another for various applications. In contrast, human beings have been using and discarding nature's resources unmindful of the load that it causes on the ecosystem. Consider the invention of Ozone Depleting Substances (ODS) like halons and CFCs for fire-fighting, refrigerant and solvent applications. These chemicals were hailed as wonder chemicals as they met all the 'human' critera of development on the industrial and economic scales. As is their wont, humans do not study the impact of such innovations on the environment as that does not fall in the 'development measuring' criteria. However, when the ozone layer depleting potential of these chemicals was realised, the 'innovative' race began all over again to find their replacements as the earlier innovation had to be discarded. Quite a few replacements of ODS are Green House Gases (GHGs) that have the potential to cause further harm to the environment. Such a methodology of development is fraught with danger.

Human beings waste most of the resources that they start to work with while creating products. Consider the following two examples:[1]

- In the pharmaceutical industry, a ton of saleable pills requires well over 150 tons of raw material.
- Coal fired electric power stations waste two-thirds of their input energy before the current starts flowing.

In that context, this chapter would study the armament usage in the IAF in order to understand if their usage for training can be optimised to extract more value from the same resource i.e to increase the resource efficiency. More than efficiency, can the IAF adopt good practices for process improvement in order to reduce the costs of armament usage i.e to reduce consumption even while not denting its operational preparedness? In other words, the endeavour would be to suggest ways by which environmentally safe practices of increasing resource efficiency and reducing consumption can be incorporated in the IAF and the Indian military.

Why Focus on Armaments?

The three pillars of the IAF are operations, maintenance and administration. The activities under these pillars are similar to those of any large industrial conglomerate. In the context of consumption of resources, the IAF can take a leaf out of any industrial organisation's working processes, learn from it and optimise the utilisation for reducing environmental impact. However, there are a few differences too between the two set-ups. Being a military organisation, one of the input resources in the IAF is the armament inventory that is procured, held in reserve and trained with, for building operational readiness. This usage is very different from any other resource that an industrial hub, akin to the IAF, would use. Additionally, the life threatening element, all-time preparedness and ruggedness of work also differentiates the IAF's work from others. Hence, it would be challenging to concentrate on these issues here, while focussing on resource optimisation, rather than on the largely industrial processes for which many examples and studies are available for emulation.

Armament usage also causes a direct and large impact on the environment. This is due to the particular nature of resource consumption that leads to release of pollutants like lead, other metal shrapnel/chemicals and harmful gases. This impact is unavoidable in wars and, thus, their usage during hostilities is not under the purview of this study. The armaments used by the IAF are costly because they do not comprise a normal industrial commodity governed by market forces. On many occasions, these are customised, and in other instances, they are manufactured against specific orders. Herein lies the leverage that the IAF holds if it wants to work towards optimising their usage and inventory management and also to lower the cost of training.

It is important to appreciate the business sense of the optimisation process being outlined here. There may be cynical responses to working for the environmental safety for the human race, on the one hand, while dealing with life endangering armament stores, on the other. However, it is a harsh reality of human existence that militaries cannot be wished away. For the militaries to function, armaments are a necessity. Since every day the militaries are not fighting a war but only training for being prepared to face it, the focus should be to reduce the adverse impact of their peace-time operations on the environment. In the process, if the cost of training also reduces, it may be called the proverbial icing on the cake.

Armaments are specific to the particular arm of the military that is going to utilise them. In the IAF, armaments are more esoteric and are commonly termed as air armaments. Since most of them are air-dropped/fired, the shape, charge-by-weight ratio, type of warhead, ballistics and method of precision guidance are some of the attributes that differentiate them from the stores used by other arms of the military. The variety of armament stores utilised by the IAF is very large and complex and, therefore, the scope for increasing their usage efficiency is equally large. Owing to the sensitive nature of the information related to the subject, this statement can only be explained in simplistic and general terms. Only those stores where the principles of resource efficiency can be applied directly, would be used for suggesting process improvements.

However, some of the armaments are meant only for war-time usage and they are obviously beyond the purview of this work.

Armament Training in the IAF

The primary aim of any air force is to guard own air space and take the firepower beyond the enemy's borders in the shortest possible reaction time. Thus, air defence and air strikes are the two force application options available with an air force and they require different types of weaponry. Obviously, for air defence, surface-to-air and air-to-air missiles are used and for strike missions, rockets, air-dropped bombs (precision or simple ballistic) and air-to-ground missiles, etc. are utilised.

"Practice makes perfect". The oft repeated adage is accurate for the professionals in the IAF too. To hone their skills, the concerned air and ground-crew constantly practice firing of air armaments. The training consists of different types of air armaments that are dropped or fired over field/air-to-ground firing ranges. For the purposes of training, either the aircraft detachments are moved to a particular location so as to undertake armament training from there or the armament is provided at their parent base. There are many operational and training issues that are factored before deciding on the location of planned usage of the armament stores. Each aircrew has a set of armaments to be fired in a year. This is based on a set formula that works out the numbers of specific training stores (light bombs, etc) and normal armaments (that is, the same as war-time stores) that would be used by each aircrew. It is obvious that the bottom line in this training is gainful use of experience, similar to war-like situations, for all the personnel involved with this usage.

In line with the need of the military organisation, each combatant member of the IAF also has a set quota of Small Arms Ammunition (SAA) that he/she has to fire in a year to remain adept in the use of small arms like revolvers, rifles and light machine guns. This quota has been fixed keeping in mind the stage of training of the combatant member, and normally plateaus out after initial training is completed. The quantity of ammunition also varies for different branches of the Service. This firing training is carried out in each major formation of the IAF, at the ground firing ranges (called small arms range). The lead that accumulates due to firing of ammunition, in the butt of the ground firing ranges, needs to be collected (to the extent possible) and disposed of periodically through logistics procedures. If this exercise is not carried out periodically, it is likely to cause ricochet when more and more firing is undertaken at the spot having the embedded lead. The lead then also poses a danger of seeping down to the ground water over time and contaminating the same. This phenomenon has already reached serious proportions in the US. Consider the following statistics and set of information[2]:

- According to the US Environment Protection Agency's (EPA's) Best Management Practices:
  It is estimated that approximately four percent (4%) (80,000 tons/year) of all the lead produced in the United States in the late 1990s (about 2 million tons/year), is made into small arms ammuntion. Taking into account rounds used off-range, and rounds used at indoor ranges, it is clear that much of this 160,000,000 pounds of lead shot/bullets finds its way into the environment at ranges.
- EPA – Best Management Practices states the following site characteristics that may lead to increased potential for lead pollution:
  - Lead reacts more readily and may become more mobile under acidic (pH < 6) conditions. In general, soils in eastern US tend to be acidic.
  - During and after periods of rain, storm water runoff may wash lead particles or lead compounds off the range. If there are surface water bodies such as lakes, rivers, or wetlands in the down-gradient, the potential for the lead to adversely affect the surrounding environment is even greater.
  - On-site or contiguous surface water bodies: very high potential for contamination when shot fall zone is located over, or adjacent to, water; increased wildlife exposure; increased lead dissolution.

The way this issue is handled in the IAF has already been covered in the second chapter wherein the waste disposal methodologies have been studied. This issue has been mentioned here to highlight one more way in which armament usage can adversely affect the environment. It is reiterated that the way forward on the subject is not banning the usage of armaments as that would be totally counter-productive to the central theme of the military. However, the right way would be to manage these assets by increasing their usage efficiency while appreciating their environment impact potential and mitigating the same.

Inventory Procurement and Classification

The armament stores procured by the IAF can be classified based on their origin – indigenous or imported. Mostly, the specialist stores received with a particular aircraft as part of a package or otherwise are bought out. In addition, there are armament stores that are role-specific owing to certain features of precision and other complex capabilities that are required to be procured from a few manufacturers of such stores abroad. Normally, while procuring these stores, their actual and extendable life is an important feature that determines the quantitative requirements over a period of time. Obviously, the complexity of the store, its contemporary technology and life play an important part in determining the cost of these stores.

Indian ordnance factories also produce many types of air armament stores. These are the older generation of air-dropped bombs and training stores. They have also started manufacturing propellants for a few air applications. The manufacturing standards are fairly dated although attempts have been/are being made to raise the quality and manufacturing standards. India also has an armament Research and Development (R&D) establishment, the Armament Research and Development Establishment (ARDE) at Pune[3], which has undertaken many indigenisation and new development projects. The IAF buys a lot of its munitions from the ordnance factories.

Considering the above scenario, it would be natural to assume that a synergy should exist between the two processes of procurement. Hence, the latest technology in the armament field, that is available internationally, should find its way to the R&D establishment and, finally, the shop floors of the ordnance factories. If this was to take place, India could develop its own ways to increase the efficiency of material use and reuse, which would optimise the armament inventory. More of this would be described later when the ways and means of optimising the armament inventory are considered.

As with most military procurements, armament stores are procured for reserves to be used in war, and for training during peace. While some of the stores are physically different, depending upon the intended purposes (war or training), the IAF normally does not differentiate between the types of armament stores required for different end uses. This is a standard practice with many militaries of the world. This methodology is fairly well thought out considering that training has to be carried out as close to the real-time scenario as possible and, thus, the same stores would provide the 'right feel'. The older stores that are nearing life expiry are, thus, used for carrying out the training, and the principal of 'First In, First Out' (FIFO) is used for using up these stores for training. Thus, training and inventory management (to avoid life expiry) are very closely interlinked for armament stores. They acquire a different hue when it is considered that armament training is a very elaborate exercise, with deadly adverse consequences of a wrongly planned move, whether in the air or on the ground.

Optimising the Inventory

After understanding various facets of armament procurement and training, it can be appreciated that the FIFO principle is of the utmost importance to derive the maximum value out of these costly stores. In its absence, the costly armament stores would life expire and then need to be disposed of without extracting any real value out of their procurement. **Since the disposal methodology of armaments is still mostly through demolition of stores, the adverse environmental impacts of disposal and usage are the same**. Judicious utilisation of resources would necessitate that the stores are not allowed to life expire but are fully utilised for training before that takes place.

Application of FIFO in the context of armament training and inventory management presents a challenge to most of the militaries. This is due to the fact that these are stored in diverse locations and required in still varied places. Their usage is dependent on the operational training requirement and availability of air-to-ground ranges[4]. Thus, practically, the oldest stores in the IAF inventory may not be available at the location where they are required to be fired from. Actual usage would require careful planning to reconcile many variables of aircraft and range availability, flying/operational environment, movement of stores at the right time and with the right mode of transport. The principle has to be applied at the organisation level and the training programme has to be designed by the Service HQ keeping this in mind. Thus, the oldest stores in the entire organisation should be allotted and moved for training purposes in the first instance even if they are available at a far off location. For operational reasons, if it becomes imperative to utilise some of the stores from the same or nearby location (from which the aircraft are operating), then it would be prudent to apply the principle at least at the regional HQ level. Therefore, the oldest stores in that region should be allotted and moved for training when the aircraft operation is taking place in that particular region. It is to be understood that this should not be treated as a standard practice or used as precedence. To follow the FIFO principle on the stores already available at the location of aircraft operations would obviously be the easier option but totally incorrect.

There is another way of ensuring reduction in the cost of armament training and its environmental impact. It has been mentioned earlier that armament training requires using actual combat stores to generate a realistic training environment. During the time of procurement, it is well known that some part of these stores would be required for training purposes. Therefore, if some proportion of these stores can be so customised as to be filled with less explosives, having the same shape, weight and ballistics characteristics, then their usage during training would not adversely impact the environment. The impact of using high explosive bombs on the environment can be gauged by comparing the figures of explosives filled in the low explosive bombs with those filled in a normal combat high explosive bomb. Both would be dropped by air and would show the same aerodynamic properties owing to similar design and weight. A high explosive, air-dropped bomb anywhere in the world, weighing about 500 kg, would have 40-45 percent (by weight) explosives. In comparison, a low explosive bomb would have only 10-15 percent or even less explosives. If a training mission requires only validating the homing/navigation of an armament store, it would be prudent to utilise a low explosive or even inert store.

There are various options available for dealing with combat stores as they approach their shelf life. These are listed below in the desired order of priority of their implementation.

- If the life of the combat stores can be extended after periodic change of explosives and other lifed components, then this may be the best course of action. Not only would this save cost on future procurements but also help the environment by reducing consumption of resources.
- Another change that can be brought about in the combat stores is to modify a few of them for training at the time of their life expiry. Changes like instrumentation of the combat missile for using it for training missions at the time of life expiry is possible and may be resorted to in consultation with the Original Equipment Manufacturer (OEM). However, deciding on the actual proportion of stores to be modified for training at the time of life expiry would require adoption of a long-term perspective on training with regards to that particular armament store.
- There would be some combat stores that would still approach their life expiry period. These would be available for training in as-it-is condition and should be used so in order to achieve the full value from their procurement.

Fig 3.1: Optimising Bought-out Armament Inventory

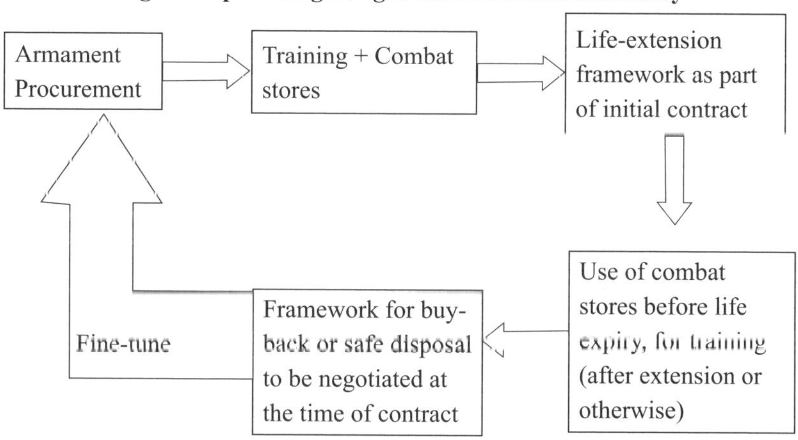

Customisation of stores for specific training needs and extending the life of combat stores can be easily undertaken if their manufacturing has been indigenised as the changes can be easily incorporated when the technology is available in-house. This raises two pertinent questions: (i) what drivers can be used to ensure that the bought out stores can also be life extended or gainfully utilised as a routine? And (ii) how can the technology for indigenisation of armament manufacturing be easily made available?

The answer to the first question is complex. This process has to be thought out at the time of procurement itself and made incumbent on the supplier. This would involve engagement with the OEM over the life span of the stores. As a business practice, it is considered desirable by both, the suppliers and the customer, to remain engaged over the life span of the product. When the armament store is decided to be purchased from abroad, the initial contract for procurement needs to encompass a framework for the following:

- Explicitly seek the framework of life extension after the initial life expiry, duly recording the changes that would be required, along with the cost enhancement.
- If combat life extension is not possible any further or has been fully utilised, then seek the framework of methodology to extend life with a view to use the stores for training purposes.
- If incorporation of training life is not possible or achieved, then the user should seek the safe disposal methodology of life expired stores from the OEM, either by removing the explosives and safe burning (instead of demolition) or any other environmentally friendly means. Including a framework for buy-back of the store after life expiry may also be one option that can be exercised at the time of procurement itself.

The Indian Defence Procurement Procedure (DPP 2006 and later)[5] makes it necessary to execute offset projects by the suppliers for projects of a certain value, in addition to a few other conditions. Amongst the list of defence products that are covered under the offset policy, armament stores are covered prominently. So with regards to the second question posed above, one of the best sources for infusion of the latest armament technology into the country could be the offset route. This would require minor changes to the DPP but benefit the Indian Ordnance Public Sector Undertakings (PSUs) a great deal. This technology can then be gainfully utilised for the tasks that have been envisaged above (life extension, converting combat to training stores, etc.), for the bought out stores.

To some extent, recycling by increasing life with replacement of explosives is already being done for some of the older generation stores by the ordnance factories in India. The need of the hour is to make this a standard practice for as many stores – bombs, rockets and missiles – as possible, without depending on outside support. This would be possible if the technology for the same is imbibed at the earliest. This technology would not only include the chemical process, quality and testing techniques but also the latest methodology involved in the manufacturing of explosive structures. The era of mixing explosives in buckets in factories should finally be a thing of the past. As an example the latest explosive technologies are even breaking the chemical boundary by creating lead free detonators so that they have less impact on the environment.

Futuristic Armament Training

We are witnessing rapid technological changes taking places in air power force application. The weapon delivery platforms are witnessing a generational change and the modern aerospace powers of the world can be said to be at the doorsteps of the 'five plus' generation of hardware. Stealth, network-centric warfare, data overload and computer algorithms deciding weapon release timings, are some of the changes that are transforming the air power projection. In such scenario, the armament training has also got to transform to keep pace with the technological changes taking place. It would be a costly proposition to fire scarce weaponry to gain hands-on experience for each aircrew. This brings us to the concept of quality over quantity. While the need for proving the weaponry and some amount of hands-on experience cannot be denied, the IAF has to seriously consider the use of advanced armament training simulators that can create a virtual battlefield of the 5th generation. Such simulators are already available globally and need to be customised for the IAF's operating scenarios and can integrate Virtual Training Simulators (VTS), with the option to choose different terrains for practising different armament usage. This would in the normal course, reduce use of armaments for training missions and would be very cost-effective in the long run. Even maintenance simulators that allow for training of ground crew on armament handling and fusing activities, should be procured and extensively utilised. The need of the hour is to show confidence in such methodologies and convert a percentage of flying effort towards such environmentally friendly, but effective, practices.

Another paradigm shift that can prove very effective is applying the principle of 'need based training' while dealing with armaments. This is already being implemented in the IAF to a large extent wherein a graded syllabus is executed for the aircrew. The concept can be appreciated when considering the efficacy of training with older armaments whilst using the latest military hardware. This may require an overhaul of training patterns. Consider another example wherein all types of small arms training is imparted to each combatant member of the military. It is true that every member of the military is required to be conversant with all types of small arms and ammunition. Therefore, they are authorised to fire a fixed quantity of ammunition of all types each year. If this quantity is the same for each combatant member, irrespective of their domain of operation, then there is a need for introspection. If the military officers are required to use revolvers predominantly during combat and rarely use other types of small arms, then training them at the same level as others who would mostly use other firearms may not be warranted. This is not to say that personnel should not be conversant with all types of firearms but the degree of expertise should depend upon the envisaged need. It may even be argued that for developing expertise on all types of small arms, increased need-based use of small arms simulators may be considered. These simulators are now readily available off the shelf. Actual firing training may be done on the types of arms where combat experience is a must and for all others, only minimal actual training carried out, with the desired expertise built through use of small arms firing simulators.

Disposal of Life Expired Munitions

With the aforementioned recommendations, it is envisaged that there would be a limited need for disposal of armament stores whose life expires before they are gainfully utilised. Holding of life expired munitions is not safe due to deterioration of the chemical properties of the explosives filled in them. Thus, these stores would have to be disposed of. At present, such stores are disposed of by Open Demolition/Open Burning (OD/OB), thus, adversely impacting the environment. Disposal of unwanted munitions, rocket motors, and other explosives by OD/OB releases a huge quantity of toxic chemicals into the environment and shakes buildings far away from the blasts. Safer disposal methodologies like, for instance, removing and gainfully utilising the nitrogenous explosives by converting them into fertilisers, can be perfected in consultation with either the OEM or experts in the field. This approach may reduce many man-hours, armament associated risk and highlight the military's environmental leadership.

Environmentally safe disposal techniques of armaments may be worked out only in consultation with the OEM. If it is made incumbent on the supplier to take care of disposal of life expired stores, then it would be a win-win situation for both. This could be done as a buy-back option and a framework negotiated at the time of procurement of the stores. The supplier may then be able to utilise some part of the stores before actually disposing of the remaining portion and, thus, recover the cost involved in buy-back. Also, the users would have been spared the onerous task of disposal on their own accord.

As an alternative to the process suggested above and as an interim measure for legacy stores, the concerned military organisation may approach the OEM to suggest ways to safely dispose of them. The OEM may be in a better position to guide the users on safe disposal, having designed the stores themselves. They may even be interested to retrieve a certain portion of the stores and pay for the same even while working towards the environmentally desirable activity of waste reuse. This process does not find favour with the users as it involves discussion on life expired (and, thus, inconsequential) stores. Correct environmental orientation of the organisation should make this a priority.

Recycling of armament stores, by the use of the old shell or casing of the stores and changing the explosives, has already been mentioned earlier under the section on Optimising Inventory. This practice is effective wherever the life of the casing so permits. In case the life of the casing can't be increased, it would be better to recycle the metal case after removing the explosive safely.[6] OD of armament stores should be considered the last alternative for their disposal. It is unfortunate that presently this method remains the first way of disposal of armament stores even in modern military organisations.

Management of air-to-ground firing ranges where the armament training is carried out is another area where environmental concerns can improve the working conditions of communities in the vicinity. First and foremost, it should be appreciated that these ranges are used for heavy aircraft fired/dropped munitions. The safety distances that are mandatory for ensuring the safety of communities in the region have to be strictly enforced. With more and more pressure on real estate due to the increasing population in India, this is fast degenerating into a dangerous situation. The encroachment near these ranges needs to be curbed by effective governance. The local government has to be alive to the situation to ensure the safety of the local population.

The recovery of shrapnel from these ranges is also of paramount importance to ensure that this does not cause ground contamination. The IAF has well drafted procedures that allow for outsourcing the waste collection from these ranges. Since higher waste retrieval implies a higher cost advantage to the contractor, it is normally ensured that much of the shrapnel is retrieved. The military has a responsibility to ensure that the outsourced waste retrieval job is performed with due safety and under authorised labour laws on their ranges even though the labour is employed by the contractor. These details should be built into the outsourcing contract so that it becomes legally binding on the contractor.

Armament Safety and Storage

While discussing armaments and their environmental impact, it is important to consider their storage and transportation conditions as these directly affect the life of the stores. Most of the precision stores require special conditions of storage (like controlled temperature and humidity) and restricted mode of transportation. When stored in a non-controlled environment, the life of the stores decreases drastically and their performance also becomes suspect. Transportation by road or train and by air, affects the life differently as the filled explosives are likely to deteriorate when transported over an uneven surface. There are specific guidelines on the safety of armaments, during storage and transportation. These are issued in India by a department under the Defence Research and Development Organisation (DRDO). While safety is the paramount concern, the military also has to ensure that the life of armament stores is not wasted on avoidable transportation and storage in non-controlled atmospheric conditions. The development of infrastructure to store the armaments should be given as much importance as the military hardware itself. After all, the military hardware would be rendered inconsequential if the armament for delivery is not available or serviceable. Thus, it is essential that a precious resource like armament is so treated as to avoid unnecessary life expiry that would directly impact the operational and training capabilities of the military and also use up precious natural resources.

Lean and Mean Military

Financial pressures are being faced by almost all countries. One of the expenditures that any nation is reluctant to reduce, even marginally, is the expenditure on defence, due to the sensitivities involved with national security. In such a scenario, it is essential that the military establishment appreciate its responsibility and use the resources put at its disposal, judiciously. Since armaments comprise a critical resource for any military organisation, their optimum utilisation would not only make economic but also operational sense. Management of the armament inventory is a complex process because it does not follow all the essential parameters of a traditional industrial resource but is still the most essential element of a military's existence. Its environmental impacting potential is also one of the largest. To study armaments as a part of the resource efficiency drive, for furthering the cause of the environment, is a difficult but essential connect to make.

Optimising the armament inventory has to start at the time of the initial procurement contract itself. Distinguishing and amalgamating the combat and training armament stores at different stages of their life is a complex process that has to be performed by the operators with a high amount of accurate planning. While some part of the inventory should be procured as training stores at the time of the initial contract, there might be a requirement to convert the combat stores to training at the time of their life expiry. Some combat stores would still get life expired in storage due to the peculiar nature of the inventory and the need to store them as war reserves till the end. These stores would need to be disposed of in the most environmentally friendly manner in consultation with the OEM. The militaries normally resort to open demolition of the stores. This causes the same adverse affect on the environment as actual firing of the store, with no value derived from it. Thus, this state is to be minimised to the least possible and to do so, the practice of following an organisation specific FIFO principle for training stores needs to be adopted. The option of safe disposal of armaments, like buy-back, after life expiry, needs to be explored, to derive maximum value from the product. The flexibility available in managing the inventory increases manifold if the production line is indigenised. The need of the hour is to invest in transfer of armament technologies mostly under the offset clause of the DPP. This would lead to long-term gains and is strongly advocated in the Indian context.

Training on armament delivery is an integral part of the military's operational readiness. There are ways by which armament training can be modernised without actually firing of these stores. Realistic simulators are available, allowing for an actual feel of the armament stores, whether on the ground or in the air. The provisions of new defence procurement policies should be suitably modified to facilitate procurement of this training hardware. In the long run, this would prove cost-effective even while building the operational capability of the military.

Preserving the life of the armament stores by the correct storage and transportation practices is of the utmost importance. This is not only essential for the safety of the stores, and, thus, the personnel working with them, but also for ensuring that they are available for their full intended life.

Non-utilisation, early life expiry, accidents, and inadequate training on the armament are all causes for concern and cry out for optimising the resource, in line with what has been suggested above.

Notes

1. Gregory Unruh, *Earth, Inc. Using Nature's Rules to Build Sustainable Profit* (USA: Harvard Business Press, 2010), p. xii-xiii.
2. This information has been taken from http://noflac.org/accessed on April 13, 2011.
3. For more information, readers may visit http://www.drdo.gov.in/drdo/labs/ARDE/English/index.jsp?pg=homebody.jsp
4. For more on non-availability of firing ranges, reader may refer to the news article at this site, http://economictimes.indiatimes.com/news/politics/nation/army-faces-dearth-of-firing-ranges/articleshow/7759709.cms, accessed on May 3, 2011.
5. For details on the subject, readers may visit http://mod.nic.in/dpm/welcome.html, the official website of the Indian Ministry of Defence.
6. For more on safe recycling of armament store casing, please visit http://www.aria.developpement-durable.gouv.fr/ressources/34585_vierzon_ih___anglais.pdf, accessed on May 6,2011.

4

Training Future Environment Leaders

The single biggest way to impact an organization is to focus on leadership development. There is almost no limit to the potential of an organization that recruits good people, raises them up as leaders and continually develops them.

— John C Maxwell,
Author and noted expert on leadership

Training to be a Leader

Are leaders born or are they trained/developed to become one? Nature or nurture? This question has been debated threadbare at many a forum. However, it should be adequately clear to the readers from the title of this chapter itself that the author believes true leadership comes about with suitable training. This is not to deny the fact that some people are born leaders. On the contrary, there is plentiful evidence of born leaders like Gandhi and Napoleon, to name a few, who rose to lead their followers in many a great struggle, and to victory when they were presented with the right environment. But the modern day conviction seems to believe that both these aspects of leadership – nature and nurturing – are required to mould a good leader albeit it tilts more towards trained leaders.

The root of the debate on whether leaders are born or developed is based on the way leaders are perceived in an organisation or the way they apply their leadership traits to lead a group of followers. The two ways in which leadership is exercised are: (a) by applying their domain knowledge and skills; and (b) by using traits that can influence actions. The former is known as *process leadership* while the latter is called *trait leadership*. It is now believed that while the characteristics of leadership may be learned, the skills and knowledge used by the leader are filtered through his or her inbuilt traits such as values, ethics, culture and character. So even if knowledge and skills contribute directly to the *process* of leadership, the inbuilt attributes give the leader a certain uniqueness. This is how the two theories of the process of 'leadership-building' converge and make it 'whole.' It is, thus, critical that a born leader is bestowed with suitable skills and knowledge, to be able to lead effectively. From this conviction flow the contents of this chapter. The reasons why military leaders need to possess adequate expertise on matters of the environment, have been covered in detail in Chapter 1. How this expertise can be built up by suitable training, is covered in this chapter. The intention is not to suggest any systemic changes in the modular training programme in vogue currently. The objective of this chapter is to suggest a small addition to the course contents. This addition and the way to deal with the subject of environmental and resource efficiency would be different for trainees at different levels. This aspect would be covered in detail subsequently.

Fig 4.1: The Leadership Continuum

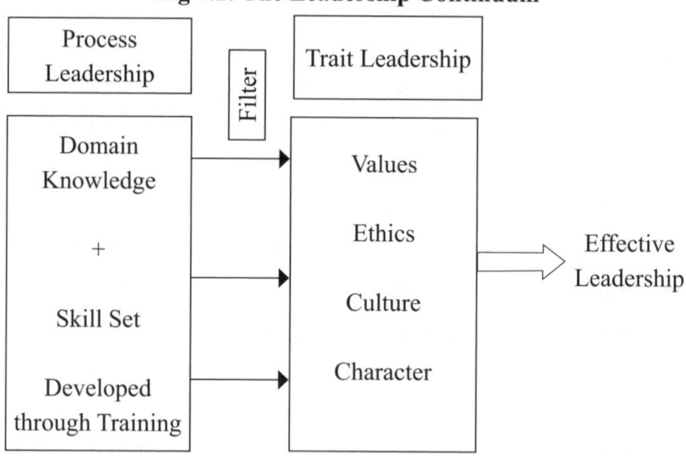

The desirability of having environmental leadership in the military establishment cannot be overlooked. Respect for resources, cost-consciousness, operational requirements and ethical/community considerations all necessitate that a military leader be aware of the environment and be able to operate in it harmoniously. Every organisation has a particular work environment, which dictates to a considerable degree how its leaders respond to obstacles and opportunities. This is brought about by the legacy of the past leaders and the thought process of its present ones. In his introductory remarks in the treatise on Military Leadership,[1] Air Cmde Jasjit has observed, "Clearly, the primary business of the soldier is to fight: and that of his military leaders is to ensure that he fights **with maximum capability and effect, with minimum costs."** The highlighted text actually dictates the envisaged training needs of a military leader. The leader has to be trained in such a manner that he can deliver on both fronts – build capability to fight and, at the same time, do it with minimum cost. Here 'cost' would apply as in the principle of war: "economy of effort" wherein human attrition has to be kept to the minimum while preparing for, and waging, war. Significantly, this aspect of economy has not found greater resonance with authors who have contributed to this work.

A vacuum exists currently in the military leadership training in terms of imparting knowledge on resource efficiency. Security is still understood as safeguarding borders while the concepts of human security are new to the young breed of military leaders in India. Knowledge is an important ingredient of leadership. The knowledge that is being imparted to future military leaders would allow them to instil similar values amongst their followers so as to mould the organisational behaviour pattern. Every contemporary military leader speaks about the subject of enhancing cost-consciousness and respect for resources amongst the personnel placed below him. Due to lack of a coherent training programme on imparting knowledge on the subject, the leader is presently not equipped to produce innovative solutions and approaches, when in a position to make interventions at various levels of the organisation. The efficiency programmes initiated by them are implemented in a stereotyped manner like 'save electricity' and 'save fuel' programmes. Even the systemic changes, which are brought about by a few military commanders on this front, end up strait-jacketing the system and lowering the overall quality of the output. Out-of-the-box thinking on building resource efficiency is difficult to come by as the present military training programme does not stress on this aspect during the formative years of the leader in the organisation, thus, not highlighting the priority it deserves.

Essentials of Training Methodology

Training is an imperative to impart knowledge, and, therefore, it has to be done correctly. Ineffective training just passes on information with no objective end-use. Knowledge may be imparted by the processes of formal and informal learning using different training methods. The terms – formal and informal learning – have nothing to do with the actual process of learning, but rather with the objectives and goals of the envisaged learning and the organisational structure that determines who gets to set these goals. In a formal learning environment, the training or education department sets the objectives; while informal learning implies that the learners themselves set their goals.

Training or dissemination of knowledge in the corporate sector is essentially carried out by a variety of methods. The training methodologies can be divided into three groups broadly, as shown below:

- Presentation method.
- Hands-on method.
- Group-building method.

The presentation method, to all intents and purposes, implies a method whereby the trainees are merely passive recipients of information. The information includes facts and processes that are passed on to the trainees through lectures facilitated by audio-visual techniques, which have become an integral part of this method in the present times. The presentation may be given by a standard trainer, a guest speaker, a student presentation or even by a panel of specialists. By the use of this method, a large amount of information is presented in an organised manner, in the least time- consuming manner, and to a large group of trainees.

The hands-on methods, on the other hand, require the trainees to be actively involved in the learning process. There are various ways in which this method can be implemented. Mostly, On-the-Job Training (OJT), use of simulators, and actual game play are techniques employed as part of the hands-on method approach. This methodology is considered a pivotal ingredient of training on physical processes that require a higher degree of skill set. Apprenticeship programmes constitute a significant part of the overall hands-on training methods. The trainer evaluates the learning process at every instance and even modifies the process as per the needs of the trainee. OJT is useful for *ab-initio* trainees or even when the skill set is sought to be enhanced by cross-training or while introducing new equipment/technology.

Group-building training methods may be used when a trainee has already undergone the basic organisational orientation programme. It seeks to improve the trainee's personal skills as well as team work. It involves sharing experiences, building a coherent group structure even while understanding the underpinning interpersonal dynamics and, thus, learning to evaluate individual strengths and weaknesses. This allows the trainee to understand the rationale for allocation of responsibilities and work within a team. This method often involves learning by experimentation. It includes learning through team activities in unfamiliar, mostly outdoor surroundings. It teaches conflict management and risk-factoring to the trainee.

Essentials of Training

Training methodologies are means to impart knowledge. To select one method over another, an appreciation of what constitutes an ideal training module is critical. While choosing a training methodology, the decision is weighed against the type of learning outcome that is being aimed for. The means adopted are dependent on the stage in the organisation at which the likely recipient of the knowledge is positioned. This is also contingent on the efficacy of the method in facilitating learning and transfer of knowledge. The training and development costs have to be evaluated so that they do not outweigh the benefits accrued from the process. Finally, the training has to be proven effective for it to sustain.

Application, end use, and conversion of knowledge into wisdom are ingredients of rightful training. Imparting knowledge for the sake of increasing the information base of the leader may be resorted to at senior positions but the same, if done for a relatively new entrant to the organisation, may prove counter-productive. Thus, application and end-use competence are two of the most fundamental desired outcomes of any training programme. To guarantee these outcomes, a tiered and modular training schedule is implemented generally. The methodology of training and knowledge contents of the module are varied for different levels of trainees as well as for different job contents. Therefore, the type of training methodology for an *ab-initio* pilot would be more of hands-on training and for an administrative officer within the IAF, the focus would be more on presentation methodology. Similarly, case study- based and role-play training methodology may be followed for a mid-level military commander but rarely for a junior level one. By now, it must be clear that drawing up a training programme consists of (a) deciding the right training methodology; (b) designing the course contents; (c) time required to be devoted for the learning imperative; (d) cost-benefit analysis; and, very importantly (e) the choice of the trainer to undertake the task. All these aspects would be covered while suggesting an effective training programme on the environment within the military, with focus on the IAF.

Training in the IAF

Before planning an intervention in an existing system, the rationale for its existence should be well understood. The IAF training curriculum is well thought out and has undergone many modifications as per the changing requirements of the organisation and for the optimisation of the human resource at different levels. At present, the officers' training in the IAF is divided into three distinct modules to suit the positional needs of its leaders. Positional need implies the learning objective commensurate to the hierarchical position of the officer at the time of training. The course contents and training format are so designed that they can be gainfully employed for professional competence and enhancing leadership projection by the officer. The focus is more on professional military and operational contents for obvious reasons and its knowledge base is sought to be augmented in the formative years of a military leader. The modular structure of the present leadership development training in the IAF is shown in a tabular form (Table 4.1). Some modules of training are common to the three Services.

Table 4.1

Organisational Position of the Officer	**Training Courses**	**Course Focus Area**	**Training Methodology**
Ab-initio Cadets/Junior Officers	At *ab-initio* training academies and other training institutes.	Introduction to Services training and development of professional knowledge.	Formal learning imparted essentially through presentation methods.
Mid-level Commander	Air Staff course at Defence Services Staff College (DSSC). Professional courses at specialist services training centres.	Developing communication and professional competence, organisational values, staff work skills and working in a joint Services environment.	Formal and informal learning, imparted through presentation methods, game play and group building training methodology.
Mid to Senior Level Commander	Higher defence management and command training at the NDC (National Defence College) aimed at strategic levels of decision-making.	To develop strategic thinking. Prepare for holding senior command positions. Enhance jointness. Develop military-civil interactions.	Presentation methods in parts. Game play and group building methodology. Through informal learning environment in most parts.

The training system in the Services is devised in such a manner that the requisite expertise and knowledge are available to a budding leader at the right time of his/her career. The knowledge is reinforced through retraining at suitable periods, depending upon the expediency of the Services. As far as the training pattern is concerned, it is modular. Even though the pattern is being modified as per the changing needs of the organisation, making changes in the course contents is a very laborious and centralised process. The professional contents are easily modified as compared to the generalised contents of training courses. This is due to the fact that the defence forces remain largely insulated from the socially pivotal issues of governance, mostly by design. Therefore, modification of the generalised contents remains a problem area, especially as domain knowledge on the subject is hard to come by in the normal course of events within the military.

During interaction with the training staff at Air HQ in July 2011, it came to light that the IAF has recently introduced the subject of Right To Information (RTI) in the course contents for *ab-initio* officers as it was felt that they need to be suitably aware of their responsibility towards such an important social issue of the present times. RTI is a subject not directly related to national security but if the leadership is not suitably oriented towards it, the consequences can be irksome and the organisation may be put in an embarrassing situation. Such changes are the need of the hour as the operating environment of the military is changing very fast wherein its personnel are repeatedly faced with social dilemmas in the normal discharge of their duties. A few examples of such interactions are: during aid to civilians at the time of disaster management operations; top leaders facing the media at public forums and when they are confronted with the country's obligation towards issues not directly related to national security. An example of the latter is India's obligations under the Montreal Protocol, to phase-out ozone depleting substances, a few of which are also used extensively in the military. Thus, they have to manage the military's operations even while these substances would not be available to them in the future. The present leadership within the military is still grappling with these issues while the budding leaders are not being trained to take decisions on such subjects.

Knowledge on Environment

The military leadership needs to evolve with the changing times. This message is loud and clear from what has been stated above. Knowledge of the environment is an indispensable part of the military's preparedness. However, the 'environment' was perceived in a more militaristic term until now to incorporate the direct security connotations of various interplays in proximity to the entity – nation/defence forces/defence personnel, etc. It did not include the physical changes taking place in the climatic environment that also had a direct and indirect bearing on the security matrix of the nation[2]. The cause and effect of climate change on the military has been well-documented. As mentioned above, a few effects are already being felt by us in the form of having to deal with the consequences of the national commitment to mitigation. A few others like control of GHG emissions would be faced by the nation in the near future; by extension, the military establishment cannot remain aloof from the measures that would be enacted by the government on this front.

To develop an environment leader, it would be necessary to arm him/her with the broad knowledge on the subject as shown below.

- **Module 1: Civic Issues**
  - Our Ecosystem
    - Green House Effect (GHE).
    - Ozone Layer Depletion.
  - Impact of different activitics on our cnvironmcnt
    - Civil life: Carbon Footprints.
    - Military activities: Carbon 'Bootprints' and Management of ODS.
- **Module 2**
  - International Environmental Agreements
    - Kyoto Protocol and its Future.
    - Montreal Protocol: Success Story.
  - National Legislation and Climate Change Mitigation Action Plans
    - Central Government Action Plans: National Action Plan(s).
    - State Government Action Plans.
- **Module 3: Service Issues**
  - Organisational Structure and Orientation on Environmental Issues.
  - Environment Change and its Impact on National Security.
  - Organisational Policies and Programmes on the Environment.
- **Module 4**
  - GHE: Mitigation and Adaptation Techniques: Future Roadmap.
    - Good Practices.
    - Green Military.
  - Tools and Techniques for Assessment of Practices
    - Environmental Audits.
    - Involvement of the Cadre.

- **Module 5**
  - Environment Change and National Security.
    - Geo-political and geo-strategic implications of environmental security.

The training modules are centred on civic and Service issues pertaining to the environment. It is necessary that a foundation is laid down before the thought- process develops towards seeking solutions on environmental issues. The overarching nature of the subject of the environment lends itself to diverse fields where its application can be made and the cause and effect studied. It would obviously not be possible to cover the entire gamut of operations within the military where the good environmental practices can be applied. It would, thus, be necessary to lay down the framework of training on the subject. Sufficient space has to be given for the budding leaders to draw their own solutions; care needs to be exercised so that the subject is not covered in such a manner that it supersedes operational efficiency or requirements and leads to a decrease in morale. This is akin to how the environmental issues are being dealt with currently in our country, almost a throwback on the licence 'raj' of yore. The basics of the subject should, thus, be covered, leaving the solutions to be brainstormed by the individual leader, depending upon the situation at hand. This brings us to the question of the position/level at which knowledge with regard to the modules given above should be imparted. The next section would throw light on this issue.

Suggested Training Capsules

The training pattern at various levels in the IAF has been covered in Table 4.1. Based on the training needs at different levels of the organisation, it has to be decided as to what modules, objectives, training methodology and actual course contents should be adopted at various levels of the hierarchy. The course contents have to be decided keeping in mind the knowledge need, absorbing capability of the mind, inquisitiveness, familiarity with the organisational ethos and, most importantly, the cost-benefit derived by the organisation while covering the subject at a particular seniority of the trainee.

Keeping the above factors in mind, it is felt that Modules 1, 2 and 3 that cover aspects of governmental responsibility/laws/legislation and the factual condition of their application in the military Services should be covered during the *ab-initio* orientation training of the young leader. Once the rudiments of the subject have been covered at that stage, they need to be revisited during retraining of the mid-level commanders. At that stage, Module 4 should also be covered in which the concept of 'green military' can be introduced. This is the time when knowledge on good practices of environment management being followed by the respective military organisations as well as other such organisations around the globe may be imparted. Involving the mid- level officers in role play as well as out of the box thinking on the subject can be encouraged for generating more solutions and developing independent thinking on such a critical social issue. The process of audit of various activities directed towards the application of environmental policies in the military would also find a place in this module. Improvements that may be accrued by the organisation once the lessons learnt during these audits are applied should be integrated in the course contents of Module 4. A major thrust area of the module would be participative training that would engage the officers in suggesting ways and means to involve the cadre in green forays. Module 5 is meant to be introduced at the NDC level or equivalent courses for one-star and above ranked officers.

Once a decision is taken on introducing different modules at a particular level of the organisation, suitable course contents need to be designed. It should be kept in mind that the field of environmental research and the geo-politics surrounding it is in a transient phase and witness to large variations taking place in a short duration. It would, therefore, be prudent to devise a course structure that may be modified in real-time as these changes are taking place. A suggested pattern of course contents for these modules is broadly described below.

Module 1

- Constitution of the ecosystem
  - Flora and fauna.
  - Essentials of life on earth – clean air, water and temperature.

- Green House Effect (GHE).
  - Green House Gases (GHGs).
  - Harmony of nature to maintain equilibrium for sustaining life on earth.
- Presence of Ozone Layer in Stratosphere
  - Protection of life on earth from Ultra Violet (UV) rays.
  - Chemistry behind formation and destruction of ozone layer.
- History of environmentalism: from ancient India to present times

- Impact of Anthropogenic Actions on the Environment
  - Industrialisation: Carbon Emissions and their impact on the increasing GHE – Carbon Footprints of various sectors – Different approaches. Scientific Debate on Climate Change.
    - Role of Intergovernmental Panel on Climate Change (IPCC): The controversy and after.
  - Global Warming: Effect on exacerbation of class differences, sea level rise, water and food scarcity and effect on national security.
    - Human security in the palimpsest of national security.
    - Recognition of the problem by the global community: History of the debate.
    - Role of the military in enhancing carbon 'bootprints'.
      - Resource consumption at what costs?
  - Use of Ozone Depleting Substances (ODS) by humans
      - Refrigeration – CFC, HCFC, HFCs.
      - Fire Suppressants – Halons.
      - Solvents – Carbon Tetrachloride, etc.
    - Use of ODS in the military – Contribution towards destruction of ozone layer – Lack of knowledge and communication gap.

Module 2

- International Efforts to Counter Environmental Degradation
  - Kyoto Protocol: Common but Differentiated Responsibility: Background: United Nations Framework Convention on Climate Change (UNFCCC)
    - Control of a few GHGs.

        - Commitment of the developed countries: Failure of the Protocol: US' inaction
        - Bali Action Plan
        - Group dynamics within the parties to the Protocol: Developed, developing and small island nation states
        - Fractured debate on the subject: Copenhagen and beyond: India's stand: Economic impact of the Kyoto Protocol on Developed and Developing Countries: Perspective during global economic slowdown
        - A brief on financial instruments under the Kyoto Protocol: Clean Development Mechanism (CDM) and its impact on India and China.
        - Adaptation needs: Funding mechanism under discussions at the international forum.
        - Sustainable development: Distant dream in the absence of breakthrough in renewable energy technologies.
            - Types of renewable energy sources in India.
    - Montreal Protocol: Need for the international agreement: An industry perspective.
        - India's commitment: Historical and present situations, National Ozone Units (NOU), Funding mechanism.
        - Situation in civil sector: Availability of halons.
        - Phase out of HCFC: Defence forces preparedness.
        - Impact on defence forces: Maintenance of legacy equipment.
        - Search for alternatives: Paradigm shift.
        - Readiness of alternatives with the industry: Reason for success.
        - Interconnection between global warming and ozone depletion and vice versa.
        - HFC inclusion in Montreal Protocol or Kyoto Protocol?: Current debate.
- Climate Change Mitigation Action Plans
    - National communication to the UN.
    - Environmental governance in India.

- Migration: Concept of 'Climate Refugees' – Internal and human security issues.
- Food and water security: Effect of global warming – sea level rise, rise in frequency of sudden climatic events: IPCC's latest report on the subject: India's take on scientific evidence on linkages of sudden events with global warming.
  - Uncertainty of timelines: Analysis of reasons for international 'complacency' on mitigation.
  - Challenge of managing agriculture with unpredictable weather patterns.
- National Action Plans: Eight Action Plans for climate change mitigation: Present status.
  - India's energy needs.
  - Implications for different states.
  - Role of Ministry of New and Renewable Energy (MNRE).
- State government action plans for Climate Change Mitigation: This subject may be covered only for one odd state such as Gujarat or Tamil Nadu as an example to inform about the role that states play in the entire gamut of policy implementation on climate change mitigation.
- Monitoring agencies and criterion for implementation of action plans at different levels.
  - Role of the judiciary
  - What is Environmental Impact Assessment (EIA)?
- Adaptation as a part of Action Plans. Need for adaptation in the Indian context. Funding as an impediment to adaptation strategy in developing countries.

The two modules described above deal completely with the social facets of environment management. This is the foundation of knowledge that needs to be laid first for a military officer. This foundation would assist him/her to draw a bridge between the policies being implemented in the civil sector vis-à-vis those in the military. There are lessons to be learnt by both the sides. Most of the civil sector, being predominantly involved with their social commitments, has well-drafted policies on climate change adaptation and environmental resilience. On the other hand, the military has few policies and directives on the subject at this juncture but their implementation, as is expected, assumes top priority and is carried out with military discipline and precision. Thus, only after understanding the national commitments on the subject and international environmental focus, can a leader fully appreciate the canvas of activities involved while dealing with the subject. Extrapolating these activities for the military would be a leadership act that would require out of the box thinking until training on a social system within the military matures. Only after the broad issues concerned with the environment are covered can the knowledge on their application and implications for the military be imparted. At that point in time, it would be crucial to inform the trainees on how the organisation perceives the issue and is geared to confront it. Imparting a realistic picture is critical. Only then, progress made on both mitigation of, and adaptation to, climate change by the military is appreciated, thereby preparing itself to understand what is still left to be achieved.

Module 3

- Military and Environment
  - Orientation of the organisation: Understanding of the environment issue amongst the military leaders – Need and application
    - Resource efficiency as the natural by-product of respect for the environment – actual case studies from the organisation.[3]
    - Management of ODS in the military.
      - Usage in maintenance and administrative infrastructure.
      - Halon banking.
      - ODS inventory management.
    - Diplomatic initiative of showcasing organisational commitment towards the sensitive and contemporary social issue of environmental protection.
  - Organisation chart of environment nodal points at all levels of the organisation. The level of interaction with other nodal agencies of the government dealing with the issue.

    - Responsibilities associated with each nodal point.
    - Training requirement for filling up specific environment-related appointments.
- Environment Change and National Security
    - Effects of global warming viz sea level rise, melting of polar ice caps, water scarcity in the 'third pole' (Tibet), food shortage, vector diseases and international pressures on reduction of energy consumption. All these would cause:
        - Climate-linked migration leading to pressures on effective governance due to enhanced class and economic disparities. Enhanced poverty levels result in internal disturbance with the poor being used as fodder for vested interests.
        - Exacerbation of international fault-lines due to paucity of water. The India-Pakistan Indus Water Treaty would be under pressure once the tributaries start drying up. Water sharing is already a major issue between India and Bangladesh.
        - Opening of sea lanes due to polar ice melting. Impact on international trade and geo-politics. Security of channels of communication. Span of operations.
        - Impact on military medical services as vector-borne diseases start becoming rampant and in new areas. Research and interaction with civil counterparts to understand the impact on one's own troops at deployed locations.
        - Unpredictable weather patterns would add another paradigm in operational planning and training.
        - International pressure is mounting on stepping up mitigation efforts by high trajectory economies like India. It is a matter of time when this is bound to culminate in increased pressure on military installations to be more energy efficient. Preparation for energy efficiency in a systemic manner without strait-jacketing the operations.
- Organisation's Environmental Policies
    - Instructions to aircraft Base Repair Depots (BRDs) on

management of halons used for filling aircraft fire extinguishing bottles.

- Monitoring of fuel consumption on quarterly basis (more for budgetary purposes).
- Waste Management[4].
  - Instructions for managing e-wastes.
  - Management of domestic wastes for furthering flight safety measures.
  - Instructions for managing industrial wastes generated in BRDs; not at the same level in operational formations.
- Participative training on deciding the future roadmap: this should be the last part of this module. Beyond these relevant aspects, the trainees may be asked to submit an assignment on how, according to them, environmental mitigation could be enhanced within the military. Coherent ideas may be suitably rewarded and forwarded for follow-up, akin to the flight safety model.

The course contents for Modules 1, 2 and 3 have been designed keeping in mind the requirements for an *ab-initio* trainee as well as for retraining of mid-level officers. The depth of the training curriculum may be suitably reduced depending upon the allotted duration of training and whether it is being used as a syllabus for retraining or for an initial training programme. However, removing any particular subject may prove to be counter-productive, so that may be avoided. Normally, these three modules should be covered in a linear manner, following the presentation method. Improvisation in the third module to include case studies and encouragement for independent thinking should be given due emphasis. This could be given more focus in the retraining phase but it is also required to be adequately covered during the initial training of the military officers.

After completing the first three modules, a military officer may be considered to be trained on environmental matters so as to take independent decisions on these issues while working in any operational environment. However, policy drafting on any matter requires a different skill set. It is imperative that a conceptual level and strategic thought process is undertaken before long-term policies are drafted. This brings us to the next module (Module 4) which is aimed at developing such thought processes at the senior level hierarchy. It is meant to prepare them for indulging in some creative thinking and implementing wide-ranging reforms within the organisation for mitigation of, and adaptation to, climate change. They would also be ambassadors of these policies and would be expected to coordinate these policies with other organs of the government. The course content for this module is described below.

Module 4

- Good Environmental Practices in the Military: Transcending the mindset
    - Requirement of overarching policy: Indian Army in the lead [5]
        - The Ministry of Defence does not have a policy on the environment.
        - Indian policy-makers still do not include human security under the umbrella of national security.
    - Concept of Green Military: Peace-time initiative
        - Top down approach for formation level policy on environment preservation is a must.
        - Green buildings: Military Engineering Services working towards it – More requires to be done.
        - Direct actions like planting trees and disposal of municipal waste are priority areas.
        - Capacity building of future environmental leaders.
        - Showcasing social commitments undertaken by the military.
        - Training commitments should be made greener without impact on operational efficiency.
    - Adaptation to climate change or consequent national action plans requires future organisational policies to be made keeping in mind the adverse impacts.
        - Adaptation not yet a priority.
- Executing Good Environmental Policies

- Need for environmental audits to check the efficacy of policies
  - Training of auditors.
  - Rationale behind setting up benchmarks on the basis of which the audits have to be conducted.
  - Environmental audit process: Use of existing audit agencies.
  - Results of audit: Reorientation of policies based on findings of the audit. The level of hierarchy that carries out the reorientation.

- Capacity building of cadre
  - Permeation of a safe environment culture within
    - Knowledge empowerment as a means of furthering the reach of good environmental practices.
      - Information on ODS: Need for its management in the organisation.
      - Information of good practices being followed.
      - Information on environment organisational structure
      - Waste disposal: Domestic and industrial.
    - Importance of rank and file to get involved with resource efficiency
      - Importance of resource efficiency as a part of good environmental practices.
      - Difference that their efforts can make in saving costs involved in operations.
      - Case study-based teaching on resource efficiency in the respective organisation.

The author is of the opinion that module 5 does not need a syllabus to be defined. The highly dynamic nature of the issue dictates that these subjects should be covered only through guest lectures at the NDC and similar courses.

At present, there is no training on the subject for the lower seniority personnel within the military. This is likely to decrease the efficacy of implementation of policies, especially if all personnel are not on board with respect to the larger operational and social gains that are likely to be accumulated by implementing these policies. With the advent of the information age, the personnel can be easily motivated once their role in achieving the desired environmental objective is explained to them. This should be the focus of any training that is conducted for the workforce. Informal training methodology should be followed initially for conveying the message of building resource efficiency leading to safeguarding of the environment. The target audience for such training would be mid-level non-commissioned ranks of the military. The message would be conveyed forcefully with the use of actual case studies that highlight how these policies would stand the organisation in good stead – operationally and to build a positive image.

Evaluation of Training

Once a training schedule and its course contents have been worked out and implemented, it would be equally important to evaluate its impact and efficacy. Since continual improvement is a desired feature of any quality system, a feedback mechanism has to be inbuilt in the system loop, to enable advancements and optimisation. Normally, this evaluation of training is carried out in the Services in the form of a questionnaire that is given to each trainee after the programme and they need to give their quantitative or qualitative feedback on each aspect of training in response – from the trainers to the course content, from the duration of the programme to the adequacy of the focus on each area. Their views are also sought on any other subject that they would like to be covered in the training. After the trainees go (back) to the operational formations, assessment of the adequacy of their training level is sought from their superior officers. This also acts as a valuable tool in the hands of the training programme planners.

With regard to training on environmental matters, it would be practical to focus on feedback from the trainees as a group and as individuals. Feedback from superiors in the operational formations may not really work at this juncture, primarily due to the limited exposure of these superior officers to environmental issues. More than the established feedback pattern being followed at the moment, it would be better to see the recall value of the course contents and its application. One way that this could be done is to ask the officers (junior to mid-level) to write a paper on the subject within six months of reaching their units. The paper should be dedicated to practical solutions to environmental problems that are being encountered or observed within their formation. Some of these papers should be selected based on criteria such as depth of the problem perceived, practicality and innovativeness of the solution found and the overarching nature of issue(s) discussed. These papers should then be brainstormed in the next course without revealing the formation's name. It would provide a good learning experience to the young leaders and prepare them to do some innovative thinking of their own. Some incentive may be provided to the best solution provider as a motivation. The type of solutions suggested would also provide feedback to the trainers on what actually has been assimilated by the trainee from the course. Improvements in the course contents as well as the knowledge imparting methodology should take into account the papers written by the former trainees as well as the ideas being generated through brainstorming on those papers. This may be treated as an immediate response and be covered in Module 3 as part of the case study. The environmental audit of a formation can also be used to examine the assimilation patterns of the trainees that have undertaken such training. Here it would be better to study the pattern rather than individual progress. The idea is not to encourage learning by rote in this field but to encourage deeper thinking of the issue. This aspect would be covered separately in detail in the chapter on 'Environmental Audits'.

Importance of Right Mix in Training

Military training has to focus on inculcating war-fighting abilities in the trainees. There is no denying that this should receive the highest priority. Growth of a leader in the military starts right from his/her selection procedure where such traits are assessed. The leader is then imparted adequate military and organisational knowledge through various training means to become a complete leader for steering the organisation. However, till recently, the training process did not include many issues related to interaction with the civil society even if they affected the working of the military organisations. This process is now being forced to change due to the growing need of the hour. There is a great need for the training to be made inclusive of contemporary societal issues like RTI, environment stipulations and media management at the *ab-initio* and mid-seniority level. Total growth of an officer can only be ensured by making the training all inclusive.

The evolution of an organisation can come about only if it invests in its future leaders. The starting point for the process is the change in the training pattern of its leaders. What has been attempted here is to suggest how the training mix can be suitably modified, to contemporise the knowledge base so as to assist in making a true leader. Only one subject of this additional mix has been suggested here: national and international environmental issues. There are some other social issues, as mentioned in the previous paragraph, that may be included in the overall training curriculum of a military officer to make it more balanced. This is the need of the hour as there are many instances wherein the military commander finds himself short on the necessary expertise and skill set when faced with social issues that are cropping with increasing regularity. This suggested training addition would not only result in making an environmental leader of the future but also make the military extract more 'value' while optimising 'effort'.

Notes

1. Air Cmde Jasjit Singh, *Military Leadership for Tomorrow* (New Delhi: Knowledge World, 2009), p.ix.
2. Gp Capt Manoj Kumar, *Environment Change and National Security* (New Delhi: Knowledge World, 2011), Ch 1.
3. In Chapter 3 of this treatise, how resource efficiency in armaments can help to increase operational efficiency, has been mentioned. Similarly, the case of eco battalions of the Indian Army can be mentioned.
4. Chapter 2 of this treatise deals with waste management in defence installations.
5. For more details, the Indian Army website may be referred (accessed on July 15, 2011) http://indianarmy.nic.in/Site/FormTemplete/frmTempSimple.aspx?MnId=Mn7z5DsNgvU=&ParentID=W4Xw5DL5Gkm=

5

Securing a Sustainable Future Through Green Procurements

We will pay for this one way or another. We will pay to reduce greenhouse-gas emissions today, and we'll have to take an economic hit of some kind. Or we will pay the price later in military terms. And that will involve human lives. There will be a human toll. There is no way out of this that does not have real costs attached to it.

— Gen Anthony C. 'Tony' Zinni, USMC (Retd.),
Former Commander in Chief, US Central Command,
writing in a report on National Security and Climate Change, April 2007,
Centre for Naval Analysis (CNA)

Part 1

Indian Air Force: 2030

It is human nature that negativity always catches attention, and fast. So to drive home the requirement of green procurement, it is felt that painting a hypothetical dark scenario would provide it the right context. The policies and explanations on green procurement would come later, in Part 2 of this chapter.

The scenario is laid out *circa* 2030 in the IAF. When the Indian Air Force started building its strength from a low of 29 Squadrons[1] in 2010, the potency of the weapon platform was the most important criterion in the selection of machine and technology. Considering its unenviable position of being surrounded by none too friendly neighbours, this was expected. The potency of its adversaries was the driving factor in its race for achieving a degree of air superiority, both in technology and numbers. Now in 2030, it had lined up a modern and cutting edge fleet of weapon platforms that constituted its 42 squadrons. The fighter fleet consists of state-of-the-art fourth generation as well as fifth generation stealth aircraft. Most of these machines were bought from abroad under Transfer of Technology (ToT) while some of them were also indigenously developed. These machines were likely to be in operation till beyond 2040.

Global warming and rising population, both, has ensured that the people of both Pakistan and China were increasingly facing shortage of grain. India's position was not too rosy either. While, on the one hand, the increase in global mean temperature had resulted in decreased grain output, on the other, the monsoon had started playing games, with a drought-like situation in one year and near deluge the next. The Indus Water Treaty (1960) between India and Pakistan on sharing of the river water of the Indus river system was under strain as there was less than half (as compared to 1960) water in the western rivers of the Indus, Jhelum and Chenab, that would go to Pakistan almost exclusively. Agriculture was suffering and the Pakistani economy was in tatters. The blame game had begun and negative propaganda in the vernacular press was vehemently anti-India. China was no better, with its northern area turned fully into a desert. It was eyeing Siberia, now almost free of ice, for its future food needs. With a such chaotic neighbourhood, the Indian armed forces were on combat readiness should the adventurism of the leaders of these neighbours lead them to reach across the borders in search of food and other natural resources.

The IAF HQ in New Delhi was abuzz with messages from its command HQ. These were mostly routine but the commonality was a report on low aircraft serviceability caused primarily due to absence of a gas known as halon (an ozone depleting substance – ODS) that was used in varying quantities as an onboard fire suppressant. Surprisingly, this gas had been banked (or under storage) for these machines from 2010 onwards (when its production stopped internationally due to the stipulations of the Montreal Protocol – for safeguarding the ozone layer). The inventory levels had been falling for various reasons even as it was known that an adequate quantity was not available in the first place for all the machines that were being procured or built with the technology dependent on halons. The military leadership had believed that an alternative would emerge in time as a part of ongoing research, and retro-fitment would be performed to make the machines suitable for the alternatives. Some alternatives were actually invented but they were not suitable for retro-fitment in legacy equipment. A few countries that had stocks of this gas are not ready to part with it, some storing it for their own use, while others were under pressure from China to not supply the same to India. A cartel like situation has emerged.

Now weighed down by a hostile geo-political environment surrounding the country, the leadership has started considering options of replacing these aircraft with non-ODS dependent machines at a massive cost even before their life expiry since they could not afford to fly the aircraft without the vital aid of a fire suppressant. There was also a proposal to approach the government for undertaking indigenous production of halons, with or without permission from the Montreal Protocol UN authorities, considering the imperatives of national security. The best course of action to be adopted in the given situation was being debated.

Another issue of significance was emerging as the IAF was getting ready for a 'Cold Start' scenario wherein it may be required to undertake surgical strikes against known targets across the Line of Control (LOC) to take advantage of the surprise element. The operation support group had calculated that they simply did not have enough precision weapons/bombs for undertaking these strikes. The inventory mostly consisted of dumb bombs that were of the make of the early 2000s. There was talk of converting these into smart bombs by strapping the required hardware, like it was done for the US Air Force around the same time as India was manufacturing these dumb bombs. There were two thought processes which were at loggerheads. One supported the idea of converting these bombs into smart bombs by a strap-on kit rather than purchasing much costlier precision munitions as finally the purpose served would be the same. The other group favoured the latter option as they felt that these dumb bombs had lived more than half of their lives and, thus, investing still more in these at this stage was foolhardy. They were of the view that such a choice should have been exercised at least a couple of decades back. Now it was time to opt for the latest technology in munitions that had much more damage potential coupled with light weight, thus, increasing the range of the aircraft carrying the same. The decision to take one of the paths at this point of time was proving to be very difficult.

Part 2

Essence of Green Procurement

Environmentally responsible behaviour is, mostly, applied common sense. To be in harmony with nature only requires taking a few extra steps, overcoming the inertia that may have become second nature in the normal way of life. Thinking of the likely environmental impact of various activities is nothing more than thinking in advance about the means to avoid wastages. In the same context, environmentally responsible or 'green' procurement is the selection of products – tangible or intangible – that minimises environmental impacts and renders the products exploitable for their entire life cycle. The word *'minimises'* has special significance here. All consumption of products has an environmental footprint attached to it. When resources are consumed at a rate faster than can be replenished by nature, the environmental impacts become adverse. Thus, if the consumption levels can be reduced, it would be the first and the best course of action to avoid adverse environmental impacts. This chapter, therefore, starts with an assumption that all procurement actions of the military that are discussed here are because they are unavoidable for the working of the military organisations. The purpose of green procurement would be lost if the product is not required in the first place and the consumption is infructuous.

This assumption on the part of the author places an onerous responsibility on any military personnel authorising a purchase on behalf of the formation/ organisation. Respect for scarce resources should act as the first check to ensure an honest appraisal of the justification for going in for that purchase. This appraisal is needed more at the formation commander level as the large purchases have many such checks and balances already inbuilt. Once this appraisal is over and the decision to procure a product has been taken, the philosophy of green procurement needs to be followed. This philosophy, though simple in implementation, needs the active involvement of policy-makers owing to its potential of adding one more variable in the comparative cost matrix of the product. This process and the philosophy behind it would be covered in detail in the succeeding paragraphs. The objective is to provide an insight into the synergy that can be achieved between operational and product efficiencies through implementation of green procurement policies.

The complexities of the modern world do not always provide the luxury of decision-making for achieving a completely desirable state of existence. This is applicable in almost all walks of life. In military procurements too, the initially required features of a product, as projected by the buyer, almost always exceed the ones that are made available and this leads to laying down a minimum standard below which the product is not acceptable. It is this minimum standard that needs to be suitably tempered with a green perspective to allow long-term viability of the equipment being procured. For example, procuring a product not based on ODS (Ozone Depleting Substances) would not expose its dependence on a banned product at a later date. This tempering needs to be done judiciously as finally the product should not become unattainable in the case of projection of overambitious and immature technological requirements. We should aim for the purchase of 'environmentally preferable' products that prevent waste and pollution. While considering a product for making procurement decisions, there is a requirement to consider environmental impacts, along with other variables like price, performance, and other customary factors. How and why these decisions are to be arrived at makes an interesting study.

Procurement in the Military

Military organisations like those in the corporate world have different tiers of procurement. However, the process of procurement varies a great deal from country to country. In India, the Defence Procurement Procedure (DPP) is laid down by the Ministry of Defence (MoD)[2]. It is meant for procurement of sensitive military hardware and munitions. The process is fairly complex commensurate with the high cost and security sensitivities involved in such procurements. It specifies policies and processes to be used for either procuring from indigenous sources ("Make") or from global suppliers ("Buy"). There are other sub-categories that allow partnerships and allied pooling of R&D, finances and technologies, etc. The bottom line remains that of *".... the overall aim of ensuring that our forces have an edge over our potential adversaries at all times – in immediate terms as well as in sustainability – will be ensured.*"[3] The Qualitative Requirements (QRs) for such equipment are laid down by the Service Headquarter (SHQ). From aircraft to armoured carriers to ships/submarines, their role-specific munitions and training simulators, etc are all procured through this route.

The next tier of procurement in the Indian military is the centralised procurements that is carried out by the designated formations on behalf of either the complete organisation or part thereof. In the IAF, these formations are called Equipment Depots (EDs) and they procure and warehouse the procured equipment. The equipment is then supplied to individual formations upon their demand. Centralised procurement is carried out to facilitate economy of scale and, thus, help in procuring good equipment at a competitive price level. The QRs for such purchases are generally laid down by the concerned directorates of the SHQ – also referred to as AHSP (Authority Holding Sealed Particulars) in some cases, and implemented by these formations placed under them. In the Indian context, the range of such procured equipment is vast, commensurate with one of the largest standing militaries of the world. It includes diverse equipment like fire cylinders, vehicle batteries, and even cloth uniforms with different shoes/boots, etc.

The third and the last tier happens to be the procurement activity carried out by each military field formation to sustain its day-to-day functioning. These procurements are at the discretion of the users and are almost always extremely price sensitive. There are no fixed QRs for such equipment and the costs involved are not very large. The range of equipment is small and is also dependent on the limitations of the local markets. The equipment/materials purchased through local procurement action are normally short life purchases that are repetitive in nature. It is, thus, extremely important to ensure that such purchases take into account the methodology or ease of their disposal after life expiry or else they have a potential to saddle the formation with this responsibility. Purchase of tyres for common vehicles, flooring material for sites, and office equipment are all normally purchased through local procurement actions. The Indian military is very well placed in this regard as ordinarily Indians are known to utilise the last bit from their resource before discarding it for good.

Attributes of a Green Product

This brings us to the next question of how to categorise a product 'green'? There are various attributes that are essential for treating a product as green when competing with a similar product range. This understanding is important because all good intentions can be undone if in the hope of a green product, the military is burdened with a product which is not environmentally friendly and that, in turn, could lead to the draining of the organisation's resources. Some of the general attributes of a green product are listed below:

- A green product would normally be produced in a manner that consumes fewer natural resources or uses them more sustainably.
- The products should consume less energy when being used. This is one component of life cycle costs that normally mirrors the green attribute of a product. A case study of the Pentagon changing its policy on procurement keeping in mind the energy costs is mentioned subsequently.
- It should not be dependent upon hazardous or toxic materials. In fact, there may be regulatory requirements in force for newly manufactured equipment being free of ODS and other banned chemicals under UN mandated international treaties. Such chemicals are banned for export and even if accepted as part of the equipment initially, would be very difficult to be replenished. Thus, not only environmental factors but also legal considerations should discourage their procurement.
- Such products are also designed to reduce the amount of waste being created during operations or at the time of their life expiry.
- It should have low maintenance requirement and should be easily maintainable. This aspect would be explained in detail in the subsequent paragraphs.
- It should offer an opportunity for reuse/recycling and a periodic up-gradation so as to avoid requirement of fresh procurement.

- A green product should not be injurious to health during the course of its normal exploitation. It implies that the equipment should not require any input that uses health-wise dangerous resources during its operations. Of course, if a product does require such an input, the manufacturer normally specifies the precautions to be adopted. But for comparing two similar products, absence of such a precautionary requirement should be treated as a positive in its favour.
- As a rule, a product that does not have a long supply chain requirement is considered green. While this may not always be feasible in military equipment owing to global sourcing, it is nevertheless a desirable attribute. A long supply chain requirement is also a hindrance for military missions even while adding to the cost of operations. It is thus, not a coincidence that the military insists on indigenous products for its supplies, wherever feasible.

Green Procurements in the Military

Resources are precious. Individuals or organisations alike are interested in value for money whenever they need to spend. Military organisations are no different. Thus, one of the primary reasons for the military to orient towards green procurement would be encumbrance-free utilisation of the procured equipment throughout its life cycle. Considering the serious implications of downtime of a military hardware, absence of this consideration has real security connotations.

One of the important indices required to be considered in green procurement is the *disposal cost* of the product. If a product is required to be disposed of in a safe manner at the end of its total technical life, then this cost is required to be added at the beginning itself. However, if the product offers an opportunity to be recycled or reused, it should go in its favour. Innovativeness on the part of the supplier and users may be useful while considering this aspect, as explained through a case study given in the box below.

Box 1

Innovative Disposal Methodology

The military is required to be potent through procurement of latest weaponry. Fire arms for ground defence are procured and replaced periodically considering the changes in technology taking place globally. The disposal of older firearms is a sensitive matter considering the potential for misuse if they fall in the wrong hands. This issue was faced by one military organisation that was using bolt action rifles and was in the process of replacing them with self-loading and much lighter rifles, having a higher range too. Normally, the beyond-repair unserviceable rifles were disposed of by cutting of their metallic components with high temperature flame and breaking their wooden parts. All these parts were then accounted for before being disposed of by weight.

Now the contentious issue was of disposing serviceable rifles by converting them to scrap, thus, spending more money to dispose of serviceable stores. A decision was taken to explore other avenues of disposal. This was a new contingency as normally such actions are handled in a routine manner through government agencies dealing with waste disposal but in the case of firearms, this was not possible.

A chance meeting with the manager of a company of a civil arms manufacturing industry and a middle level military functionary actually provided the breakthrough. It was revealed that such old technology weapons were in demand in some countries for the sports and entertainment industry and that they would be interested to purchase these for the purpose. With this input, an initiative was taken to explore this avenue and actually such weapons were disposed of to a more developed country for entertainment purposes. Such a sale is considered very improbable – selling old technology equipment at life expiry to a developed country. But when dealing with environment friendly and resource conserving initiatives, it is essential to explore all avenues and do some out of the box thinking.

The important thing to kick-start this thinking process is the existence of "will" to explore these avenues. Even in the case study mentioned above, it would have been far easier and quicker to dispose of the weapons in the standard disposal manner of scrapping them. Extracting their complete potential before retiring them requires only a little extra effort and reaps handsome gains. This aspect of procurement policy – the necessity to extract maximum from a product – needs to be adopted and showcased, for driving the vendor to actively consider it in his initial offer. At the end, if the vendor offers a win-win equipment disposal policy, it should be counted as a big plus in favour of that particular bid.

Life Cycle Cost (LCC) is another index that forms a part of comparative analysis during the procurement process. LCC is dependent on many features of the equipment, notably the operation and maintenance costs. A holistic and expanded view of LCC is mandatory as part of green procurement of military hardware. In fact, this happens to be one of the largest used indices of the 'greenness' of a product. This would be explained in the subsequent paragraphs.

Military machines/hardware are costly but beyond that there is another dimension that mandates careful selection during procurement or development. The *maintainability* of this equipment has a direct impact on its availability during training and operations. Maintainability takes into account not only the ease of maintenance but also the input resources required for carrying out the maintenance activities. The input resources consist of the human resource, tools and testers, fuel/oil/lubricants and other support equipment. These resources are a must and have to be made available whenever and wherever the military equipment has to operate. This puts an additional burden while planning combat critical missions. It is obvious that if the maintenance activities necessitate a lower dependence on such support resources, undertaking combat missions would be easier, offering a lot of flexibility. It is also a happy state of affairs for safeguarding the environment owing to reduced use of resources. This aspect is another element of green procurement that is required for both operational as well as environmental reasons. Easily maintainable equipment would most definitely be low on LCC considerations too; preventive maintenance takes away a big chunk of equipment preservation cost, thus, adding to LCC.

As mentioned earlier, LCC is a factor that plays a big role in deciding the procurement process in favour of a particular bidder. There are various software methodologies that have been developed by consultancy firms and are available for public consumption, which permit this calculation. For complex systems/equipment, the military organisation would have to develop its own parameters that it thinks would contribute to LCC. Designing the list of these parameters is of utmost importance as its comprehensiveness would be essential in ensuring that a fair estimate of future costs is available. While most of the parameters are fairly standard in LCC, the hidden attribute is normally the one that is used as a base for running a sub-system. The example of phased out halons used as fire suppressants, ODS refrigerants for cargo/ toilet compartments in bigger aircraft, specific sealing rings/components/ lubes that require periodic change, which does not match with other periodic maintenance activities, all add to LCC. While equipment running efficiency is the primary cause of low or high LCC, the frequency of planned periodic activities on the equipment itself contributes to overall costs.

It is important that the LCC criterion is used for comparison even while introducing equipment of low complexity[4]. In such cases, it would be important to do an LCC comparison between old equipment and its planned replacement. Even if the capital costs are higher due to introduction of new and cutting edge technology, then by the same logic, the LCC should be lower, otherwise the rationale for the new introduction gets slightly distorted. This is the paradigm shift that is the central theme of green procurement in the military. The primary goal should not *only be* higher operational effectiveness but *also resource efficiency.* It is also true that resource efficiency finally leads to higher operational effectiveness. While checking for resource efficiency, it is important to carry out an assessment of the environmental consequences of a product at various stages of its life cycle. This means considering the costs of transporting, storing, handling, using and disposing of the product. Consider the following example that would give one an idea of how resource efficiency has a direct impact on operational efficiency.

Box 2[5]

...The Pentagon is the world's single buyer of oil, although it is only 0.4 per cent of market....But most of this fuel is wasted, and it is starting to figure out that it's extremely expensive, in both blood and treasure, to deliver fuel to the planes, ships and land vehicles that use the fuel, because they were designed with the assumption that delivery was free and invulnerable.

> It's not. We have a whole division of people hauling oil around and more divisions trying to guard them. About half the casualties in theatre are associated with convoys. Seventy per cent of the tonnage being hauled is fuel...So the Pentagon changed its policy in April 2007. In the future, it is going to require [the contractors bidding on new military vehicles, ships and aircraft to include in their estimates] the fully burdened cost of delivering the fuel. That means that they'll be valuing saved fuel enormously more than in the past, and the prime contractors will be competing over who can make the most efficient stuff.
> Well, that's going to speed up how quickly we get those triple-efficiency civilian cars, trucks and planes, because remember that the last things that we got out of military R&D included the Internet, the Global Positioning System, the jet engine industry and the microchip industry.

Amory Lovins' words here go beyond the green procurement policies being an imperative in the military. These policies would become a precursor to civilian products emulating the leadership displayed by the military in driving such a change. The author has always felt that military procurement can be leveraged in more ways than is being done presently; to not only drive pecuniary benefits like in offsets but actually promote transfer of technology (this would be covered in a subsequent chapter) that would be beneficial for the defence and civil industry alike, finally leading to revolutionary breakthroughs in resource efficiency.

Purchase of products that are not mandated to be *used legally* is another area of concern. For example, it is now mandatory for air-conditioners and refrigerators to carry energy efficiency rating stars and also be Chlorofluorocarbon (CFC – an ODS) free. The manufacturers are legally bound by these conditions. Purchasing equipment that does not conform to these stipulations is a recipe for disaster in the offing. Going a step further, one has to be aware of similar stipulations in the making that have the potential to disrupt supplies. Taking the same example of air-conditioners and refrigerators, one has to be aware that the replacement of CFC in the short-term was Hydro Chlorofluorocarbon (HCFC). These are also now mandated to be phased out under the HCFC Phase out Management Plan (HPMP) by 2030 (for Article 5 countries under the Montreal Protocol). The freeze in production, in fact, starts from 2013 onwards, with reduction targets starting in 2015. So procuring a machine that is dependent on HCFC today would again pose a problem in the future, probably requiring retro-fitment or replacement. Such procurements are best avoided.

Another index of green procurement happens to be the ability of the product to be *recycled* nearing the time of its life expiry. Recycling for oils/rubber and similar raw material stage products is within the realm of achievability owing to the simplicity of the process. It is recycling the complex equipment like aircraft parts (or even the whole assembly) that requires some out-of-the-box thinking. This is possible if the manufacturer has designed the equipment with this requirement in mind. Again, the demand for this has to be posed by the customer, requiring cost benefits, as the equipment is being recycled. In India, middle-class families do not throw away plastic and glass bottles, as there is an incentive to sell them to the recyclers. So with the right incentive, it is possible to think of designing an aircraft whose parts can be reused later on. One of the uses of these parts could be simulators for teaching basic flying skills to new trainees. Recycling, however, does not provide for enhancing operational efficiency but which organisation would not be interested to recover some costs from throwaway equipment? This, as well as the considerations described above, are not easily includable in the procurement considerations, mostly due to organisational culture and value set. There are a few more challenges to green procurement that need to be defined so that the readers may become aware of why these have not been implemented till now, even though it makes perfect business sense to do.

Challenges Aplenty....

As already mentioned above, green procurement policies are not easily implemented within the military. This issue gains prominence when compared with similar size civil organisations; the benefits of going in for such procurement policies are common to both but the wholehearted implementation is not across the board in both set ups. Some military and civil organisations have taken it on as an essential part of their procurement actions while just the opposite mindset prevails in others. The *raison d'être* for the lukewarm response towards the same in some can be a set of tangible motives as well as another set of intangibles.

Price: The most common and often wrongly perceived reason for not formulating a green procurement policy is the old mindset that green products are mostly expensive. This used to be a big challenge earlier but as the concepts of LCC came into vogue, organisations realised that it is not only the initial capital cost that needs to be taken into account while comparing two similar products. Green product considerations give a fair idea of the fully burdened cost of a product, also taking into account the cost of non- availability due to environmental considerations. In most cases, the price differences are due to margins being created due to the small quantity order and not due to green options. Consider, for example, a costly non-toxic alternative to a cheaper toxic product; it will cost less to transport, store, handle (health issues), and, finally, dispose of. It will require less permissions, not much training for personnel, and the consequences of an accident will be greatly reduced. In the same manner, a product that allows recycling/reusability and/or has less packaging/products needing recycling would generate revenue even when life expired and reduce expenditure on its disposal. All these considerations are necessary to compare the actual price of the product. Finally, even if the green product happens to be nominally costlier, it would become cheap in the long run if it is supported in the incipient stage and if the technology is allowed to mature by providing it crucial input during the development process; large organisations like the military need to support the process by insisting on a green product as per the attributes discussed earlier. This should not be seen as an altruistic action, rather an investment into the future.

Insufficient Knowledge: When it comes to environmental matters, this is the bane of most military organisations. They have never been involved with these considerations in the past and even now it is a reluctant change overtaking them considering the reality of the present times. Thus, there is no experience, past precedence, existing standard operating procedures and trained human resource that would be able to focus the military on the benefits of a green orientation. Once it becomes aware of the benefits that may be derived from opting for green procurement, there would be no requirement for the vendors to suitably tailor the product for incorporating green attributes, as explained previously. Therefore, such products would not become available in the course of normal business development. This challenge is, thus, required to be tackled with change in organisational strategy on procurement.

Normally, there is a procurement team in the HQ that handles large ticket capital procurements. Providing them the requisite training in these matters (as per Chapter 4) is of foremost essence. Of course, the personnel dealing with procurement at all levels have to be trained on environmental matters. Even without the training, the business sense of green procurement would appeal to them; coupled with information on operational benefits, this challenge of lack of knowledge can be overcome in the near future.

The Prioritisation Matrix: This challenge would be faced by any organisation that does not have its top management inclined towards implementing green policies. This does not imply that mid-level management would not be required to be sold on the concept – only that within the military it's almost always a top down approach. So it's very important that the top echelons realise the importance of following a green procurement policy. This is easier said than done due to the hardened and set approach of the top management. Normally, their priority would be singularly focussed on obtaining a technologically superior product. The challenge lies in orienting them towards this process. However, recent procurement events in India have showcased that LCC is playing a major role in the comparative parameters in big capital purchases. Prioritising LCC and other green procurement indices explained above (viz disposal costs, legal regulations, health concerns, etc) for even less complex equipment like vehicles, clothing, fire-extinguishers, workshop tooling, etc is also required to be considered by the military echelons.

An easier approach towards prioritising green procurement within the military is to issue a comprehensive policy on the subject. It would be an ideal situation if this policy is issued by the Ministry of Defence (MoD), since only then would the policy have pan-organisation ramifications. The policy would have to be broad-based and overarching so as to cover all aspects of military procurement and not only large capital procurements. Its implementation would then be checked by the normal audit teams that visit military formations periodically. As is customary in the military, this policy would ideally percolate down the hierarchy in the form of orders and instructions issued atypical of the pyramidal structure of the military. Since the policy would be laid down by the MoD, it would be transparent and, thus, accessible to the suppliers/manufacturers. Its institutionalisation would, therefore, drive them to offer energy efficient and green products for garnering business. The template of such a procurement policy has been attempted here and is placed as an appendix to this chapter. This would have to be customised and refined further, addressing the specific requirements/concerns of the three armed forces in India. This policy also has the potential to be adopted by other ministries for their departments after due modifications.

No Alternative: Another challenge to green procurement may very well be a genuine lack of acceptable alternatives to the present product. While prioritising green procurement in the military, it has to be kept in mind that this step should not become detrimental in terms of obtaining the desired product. For example, if one of the QRs for a product makes it mandatory for the vendor to specify a disposal methodology for the product, it may so happen that a particular vendor with a superior product (than its contemporary) may not be able to bid for the same as the original design of the product had not catered to this requirement. Until green products become mandatory as per the regulations, the desirability for these can only be projected through less than the watertight features of the RFP (Request for Proposal – the invitation of bid).

It is also correct that until these requirements are forcefully projected, vendors may not automatically invest in making their product compliant with green attributes. So it's a sort of vicious circle, where the demand and supply would play out an 'egg and chicken' conundrum. At some point of time, the organisations and vendor would have to converge on certain mandatory green features of all future products and that would then remove the challenge of 'not being able to locate a suitable green product' in a particular category. Till that time, like a farmer in the field, the military needs to toil away for such products in order to gain an operational and cost edge. There has to be a concerted effort to overcome the challenge of non-availability of alternative products. Growing demand will then stimulate the development of new and better 'green' products.

Technological Gaps: Finally, all good intentions can come to naught if actually the technologies that go into the manufacturing of a product have not matured enough (for the specific case) to fulfil the requirement of being considered a green product as per the standards laid down. These technologies may be in the form of material used or the way it is used that does not conform to the green standards of LCC legal regulations – toxicity, disposal, upgradation potential, etc. The technological gaps may exist at the (a) designer end; (b) manufacturing end; (c) user end. These would be explained now separately in the succeeding paragraphs.

When a product is designed, the focus is normally on optimum and efficient output. In fact, this is the basic premise that is taught to designers during their education and further training. An optimum design is one that delivers the desired output while using material inputs commensurate with the desired standards. Now if the standards that are laid down for measuring the design parameters have not matured so as to be in consonance with the contemporary technology, there are chances of *overuse of resources, not designing for reuse and upgradation, and probably designing high-cost maintenance equipment.* All these aspects have an adverse impact on the environment as well as the LCC of the equipment. These technology gaps during design are actually highly damaging to its effective exploitation in a safe manner and, thus, need to be tackled by investing in basic R&D and in training the human resource. An effective way to avoid the designer end technology gap is to involve theorists and end users actively with the designers during the product development process. This is a difficult process for military equipment as most of it is imported in the Indian context. Thus, there is an urgent need to consider the right course of technology transfer that would assist in decreasing this gap by widening the scope of indigenous R&D. This aspect would be further discussed in the chapter on 'Technology Transfer'.

Box 3[6]

Tata Motors in India is a highly respected name for daring to make a 2000 Euro (just above INR 100,000) car – Nano. Tata introduced its mid-level sedan car Indigo some time in 2002. There was no specific mention of the type of diesel to be used with the diesel version of the car. Most of the users were in the habit of using the higher end (thus, thought to be better) diesel with additives for better mileage and burning capability and lower sulphur content. After using the car for more than three years, the company engineers noticed that the initial design of the engine was better suited for lower end (higher sulphur content) diesel fuel as it was said to be providing better lubrication to the internal moving parts. The dealers then asked the users (including the author) to change over to this type of fuel only for better performance level of the car. The car engine was probably not designed for low sulphur content diesel, which would have been much more environment-friendly. This probable technology gap at the design stage is an example of how the environment is affected due to the same.

The manufacturing end technology gap would not exist if the designers were to take proper care in specifying tooling, material and fits requirements. However, it has been observed that during the process of setting up a manufacturing line at a location geographically away from the OEM (Original Equipment Manufacturer*) the local manufacturing ethos/ culture interferes with the OEM desired requirements (some even taken for granted by the OEM), leading to wastages, infructuous material usage and generally a high initial failure rate*. The past experience of Hindustan Aeronautics Ltd (HAL) with foreign aircraft manufacturers would bear out this fact, although it is equally applicable for the civil products also. These, in turn, affect the overall availability of the equipment with adverse consequences on the military's operations and environment. These gaps are avoided, again, with the correct methodology and procedures of technology transfer with a greater understanding by the OEM of local manufacturing techniques, supply chain management, past experience and training status of the human resource and, finally, the management's understanding of the requirements for producing the desired product. Even for a product designed indigenously some of these technology gaps would creep in but are far easily overcome as a better understanding of the inherent capability exists between the designer and the manufacturer.

The technology gap at the user end is very obvious whenever the equipment introduced is far superior to what was being used till then. The usage and maintenance understanding of this technology takes time as the older habits have to be modified even after adequate training. As an example, consider a high end car with the plastic dashboard made from a different resin than what the user has experience with. If the user uses the old cleaner liquid (which he had been using for the older car), there are chances that the plastic will degenerate and become sticky and may require a premature change. The user can follow wrong management techniques based on past experience and end up spoiling the sub-systems. There are limits to what the manufacturers can specify in the user and maintenance manuals. It is here that the role of technology facilitators like servicing and standardisation agencies within the military assumes importance in ensuring that this gap is minimised to the greatest extent possible. However, even they face the same set of technology gaps when faced with induction of new technology equipment. Thus, analysis of technology transfer documents by these agencies has a pivotal role to play in minimising these gaps, leading to drafting of accurate production and maintenance schedules based on the technology documents given by the OEM. On its part, the OEM needs to provide lucid details of the technology used and desired standards of maintenance. It has to show an empathetic attitude and take into account the experience level of the user while supplying the technology document. The tendency to supply one-document-fits-all for every user, owing to cost considerations or otherwise, may add to customer disgruntlement and higher failure rate of the equipment, needing more resources for maintenance.

It may be obvious by now that the challenges to green procurement are many but they are not insurmountable by any standards. Better communication and knowledge empowerment are mostly the keys to introducing these processes in the military or any other organisation. The benefits to the organisation and the environment outweigh the teething issues that follow any change in its wake. The will of the top management towards this aspect is equally important otherwise the thought process would not get initiated. So specifying a policy on green procurements by the MoD would be the first step if the programme is to succeed. As already mentioned earlier in the chapter, this has been attempted in the appendix to this chapter.

Sustaining the Future

Environmental sensitivity may be in vogue in civilian life, but it is hard to imagine the same in the context of the military; however, this is now changing. It is being realised that being green actually results in resource efficiency and, thus, cost efficiency, both of which are desirable for a capital intensive organisation like the military. Since sustainability is desirable for the military for ensuring higher operational preparedness, a green procurement programme forms an integral part of this drive. Green procurement in the military context means that defence activities occur with minimum environmental outcomes that may place restrictions on future use of the product.

Most of the global arms manufacturers have incorporated this programme in their product line because it makes remarkable economic sense. It has been reported that the Lockheed Martin F-35 Joint Strike Fighter (JSF) programme has achieved a 75 percent reduction in hazardous materials used to support the aircraft system (a source of expenditure for the F-22). It would use chrome-free primer and sealants, water-based cleaners, and adhesive coating applications instead of paint[7]. The military's procurement of green products and services would contribute to sound management of financial and natural resources and help promote energy conservation. It has the potential to enhance and sustain military readiness through cost-effective acquisition that not only meets the regulatory requirements, but also reduces waste generation. It would also permit the military to go in for periodic upgradation of the product to maintain a technological edge over its adversary as well as avoid cost-intensive purchase of new hardware.

No organisation can hope to survive if it does not evolve with its environment. Green procurement is the latest tool that is being used by organisations for ensuring an edge over the competition. This is pertinent for any military as it helps in lowering its vulnerability due to a shortened support tail. The synergy of lower life cycle costs with lower dependence on resources can prove to be a potential game changer for the military that follows the green procurement policies. This would also ensure that the future supplies and support structure for the equipment are not uncertain, thus, providing them confidence in strategic planning. Of course, the challenges to following such procurement policies are many and they are both intrinsic as well as extrinsic to the organisation. Most of these can be overcome by changing the organisational priority set in the larger interest of enhancing operational efficiency.

Appendix 'A'

A Draft Green Procurement Policy

In their every day operations, the MoD, the three Services (the Indian Army, the Indian Air Force and the Indian Navy) and the other organisations under the ministry have the opportunity and responsibility to be environmentally and energy cognisant in their selection and use of products and services. Proper attention to green procurement will enhance the ministry's credibility and demonstrate its commitment to environmental leadership by becoming a model consumer of green products and services. Recognising the cost and operational benefits that would accrue in following a green procurement programme, the following policy guidelines are being laid down for implementation in all departments/organisations working under the MoD. This policy would broadly address both the compliance as well as management aspect of a green procurement programme in the MoD. It is envisaged that all the concerned organisations under the ministry would issue cascading instructions for implementation of this policy.

Objectives

The objectives of the green procurement policy are defined below:

- Define a green product in the specific context of each department/organisational/formation procurement programme. (Here the MoD may wish to use the material mentioned in this chapter for broadly defining a green product as per the attributes of a green product).
- Educate and train the requisite personnel under the MoD on the requirements of 'green procurement programmes', their roles and responsibilities and the benefits of purchasing green products and services.

- Increase purchase of green products and services consistent with operational commitments, efficiency and cost-effectiveness, including Life Cycle Costs (LCC).
- Procured products or services should not substantially enhance the amount of solid waste generated.
- Improve the procurement procedures of electronic equipment through inbuilt waste disposal processes.
- Provide impetus to vendors/OEMs of green products and services.

Reduce:

- Consumption of petroleum products and explore means to increase the use of alternative and renewable energy sources.
- Use of ozone depleting substances and hazardous and toxic chemicals.
- Consumption of natural resources.

The Framework

The heads of the three Services and other organisations under the MoD would ensure the following:

1. Implementation of sustainable environmental practices, including acquisition of environmentally preferable, energy-efficient and cost-effective products. While considering cost-effectiveness, life cycle costs are to be invariably considered. It is also required that the environment impact assessment of a new product being introduced in the organisation is performed so as to realise the operational implications of introducing the equipment. This would be applicable for large equipment purchases.
2. In terms of paragraph 1 above, sustainable environment practices would mean resource efficient products, which lead to greenhouse gas emissions reduction, reduced dependency on petroleum products and low waste generation and high reuse/recycling/upgradation potential.
3. Reduction or complete elimination of products that use toxic/hazardous/banned chemicals, including ozone depleting substances. In this, it is essential that rules and regulations specified by the Ministry of Environment and Forest (MoEF) are specifically followed. The MoD

would, in turn, liaise with the MoEF to understand and disseminate to all concerned the new regulations that have the potential to impact the military operations and ongoing R&D efforts.

4. Include the features mentioned above in desirable Qualitative Requirements (QRs) of products being procured under capital and revenue heads. To the extent possible, even day-to-day purchases should also follow the principle of resource efficiency.
5. All defence buildings would follow green norms so as to be sustainable and energy efficient. However, the military buildings' design would continue to be governed by operational considerations but where possible, energy efficiency processes should be introduced. Liaison with specialists (government or private) on the subject would lead to innovations and would be encouraged.
6. It is obvious that a green procurement programme would not succeed if the personnel required to run it are not trained in it. Therefore, their training on green procurement would be organised at the think-tanks associated with defence and environment. Wherever adequate expertise is not available, training with reputed consultancy firms may also be carried out, mostly as an exception.
7. Transparency has to be the benchmark for all defence procurements.. To in-build transparency, it would be mandatory that all Requests for Procurement (RFP) documents being sent to the vendors specifically mention the requirement for the product to showcase its green attributes and that the same would be considered during evaluation of the bids as a part of LCC and otherwise too. This is likely to spur the market for green products.
8. All procurement documents of the MoD like the Defence Procurement Procedure (DPP) and similar guidelines issued for delegated procurement action, should be suitably amended to incorporate this policy on green procurement in totality. The roles and responsibilities of each functionary in the procurement chain of command would have to be specified with regards to implementing green procurement methodology, especially while comparing green attributes in the bid documents.

9. In the event a product has to be purchased for operational reasons that actually do not satisfy some criteria of a green product, this aspect is to be duly noted by the proposing officer and cleared by the competent authority who is authorised to clear the purchase in the first place.
10. It would be the responsibility of the senior management to establish procedures for an annual review of the effectiveness of the green procurement programme in the concerned organisations and departments. The senior echelon should review the procedures comprehensively to ensure continued suitability and effectiveness in meeting green procurement requirements and to ensure continual improvement in performance.

A green procurement programme is essentially a resource efficiency enhancing methodology that is expected to result in substantial cost saving in the long run and overall improvement in operational preparedness of the military. It would also focus on the defence R&D agencies to develop green technologies to decrease the country's dependence on foreign countries for importing the same. Since it may not be clear to many as to what constitutes a green product, it would be better to keep it in mind that a green product would essentially be one that would have lower dependence on extraneous resources, be energy efficient, with lower LCC, and be free of toxic chemicals.

Notes

1. A squadron of aircraft normally consists of 16-18 aircraft.
2. For more information on the Defence Procurement Procedure, readers may refer the Ministry of Defence website at http://mod.nic.in/dpm/welcome.html, accessed on November 3, 2011.
3. http://mod.nic.in/dpm/DPP-POL.pdf pg 2, accessed on November 3, 2011.
4. http://www.epa.gov/epp/pubs/grn-pur/green-pur-ems2.htm#enviropol-pent, accessed on October 31, 2011. This is from the USEPA site where they have mentioned about how to incorporate green procurement as a part of the Environment Management System. The examples given are from various federal departments.
5. Amory Lovins, Co-Founder, Chairman and Chief Scientist, Rocky Mountain Institute, Colorado, US, quoted in Gwynne Dyer *Climate Wars* (UK: Oneworld Publications, 2011), pp. 130-131.

6. This case study is based on the author's discussion with the authorised dealer of Tata Motors in New Delhi, October 2008.
7. http://www.sustainability.army.mil/tools/programtools_green.cfm, accessed on October 17, 2011.

6

Technology Transfer: Green Confluence

Perhaps my greatest omission is the military, whose use of fuel is – depending on how you look at the problem – either very hard to address or, on paper, very easy. The supersonic jet, for example, is possibly the most environmentally damaging technology ever developed. There will never be an eco-friendly F-35 Joint Strike Fighter. If planes like this continue to be deployed, they will destroy the climate as effectively as they destroy their targets.

— George Monbiot

George Monbiot wrote these words in his widely acclaimed and brilliant book *Heat: How to Stop the Planet from Burning*[1]. He goes on to say that in his opinion, the best way for the military sector to contribute in reducing carbon emissions by 90 percent is to reduce its size. He says this in the context of the UK, which does not have any aggressive neighbours. He also mentions that if he has to deal with the military sector on the subject of reducing carbon emissions, he would need to write another book.

His suggestion for reducing the strength of the military in any hot spots of the planet like South or East Asia would mostly be met with derision and knowing sneers. However, his mention of "development of climate (or environment) harming technology" for the military evokes another set of thoughts. How is military technology developed and transferred across a national boundary? Has all military technology including the internet, harmed the climate? If we want a really simple answer to this question, then it would be plainly 'Yes' but with a caveat that it is equally applicable for most technologies in the industrial era. Why single out military technology separately? If the human race were to be in the Stone Age, there would be no anthropogenic contribution to carbon emissions. But this does not mean that the military machinery cannot be as efficient as the envelope of futuristic technology allows; contributing as little as possible to carbon emissions and overall being resource friendly. Reducing the military strength or rather having a peaceful planet with no need for a military would be an ideal state of affairs. If that state is possible, then there is no need for this work. So the basic premise (and which is a reality) for writing this chapter is that militaries will exist in this world and will be required for maintaining peace. Technology development and transfer would be necessitated in their context, to maintain symmetry so that deterrence to war is available. It is but obvious that reducing dependence on resources or optimising their usage by any means – by reducing consumption (downsizing) or enhancing efficiency (discounting the Khazzoom-Brookes postulates[2]/rebound effect) – is the need of the hour for any organisation, military or civil. This would be the need for any futuristic military as well as green technology and this 'confluence of technology' needs to be studied as technology transfer, or barriers, in one sector would obviously affect the other.

With this background, this chapter would strive to study the Transfer of Technology (ToT) mechanisms that are used by the military in the Indian context. While technology transfer is being studied, the process that leads to technology development would automatically have to be dovetailed in it as that is the genesis of the transfer. The types of technology transfers and barriers in terms of denial regimes and systemic shortcomings would be an area of interest while analysing the Indian (un) success story in this area.

Confluence: Green and Futuristic Technologies

The oft repeated cliché that 'necessity is the mother of invention' holds good for any technology development and, in fact, the entire evolutionary process in nature. Since the era of world wars, military managers have access to a wide array of the latest technology. They have learnt to harness the development of science in their favour. It would not be wise to surmise, however, that technological changes have been fostered only by war-time considerations; albeit that has been a positive forcing but not a centre-piece. The military has many occasions to interact with social institutions and this interaction causes influence and counter-influence on both. Society impacts technology development and in the same vein, technology development has a modifying effect on societal behaviour. Thus, it can be seen that the process of technological development for the military and civil applications is interrelated. The rapid strides in information technology have found resonance in both sectors. The developments in space technology – for launch of satellites or the satellites themselves, have military (missile technology) and social development dimensions. The first early warning and reconnaissance satellite for the military was launched in the 1960s, and thereafter their capabilities have greatly expanded in both spheres of operations. From these developments came the terminology of 'dual use technology'. Now the future of technology development would increasingly display concern for the prevailing social construct, well beyond the narrow bounds of battle superiority. Profit maximisation would increasingly be seen as a resource optimisation tool, with environmental concerns seen as a strategy to make more dependable and efficient hardware.

Technology development for futuristic applications is a long-term strategy decision that has both economic and geo-political dimensions. In the US, the defence R&D obtains one of the largest spending for the purpose of research. In 2007, the US defence budget was $440 billion. Out of this, the technology development component was $73 billion (a little less than spending on procurement, of $84 billion). As compared to this, the largest non-military research funding goes to the National Institute of Health, which got $28 billion in 2007[3]. It is but obvious that defence R&D forays in the US would see synergetic developments in related civil sectors too and therefore, the high investment would be justified. Technology development is increasingly becoming a function of a nation's economic muscle. For a country like India, economic development has yet to see a commensurate strategy of developing dual use technology. This has to be a well reasoned venture and has to be differentiated from scientific work to application-based research, decreasing the need for future technology transfer for India.

Future technologies that hold the most promise in environment-friendly applications also have military applications and this increasing convergence is unavoidable owing to similar end requirements of efficiency and optimisation. It is also seen that the kind of technology denial regimes seen for military applications are matched only by the reluctance of the developed countries to allow green technology transfers as evidenced by the climate change negotiations of the United Nations Framework Convention on Climate Change (UNFCCC) at Cancun (2010) and Durban (2011). There are no easy solutions to the ToT, issues especially where genuine Intellectual Property Rights (IPR) barriers are also involved. Even if ToT for some lower end green technology is agreed to (like in the case of waste to energy conversion, etc), the confluence technology (green + military) would definitely see many hurdles in transfers across national boundaries. It is here that India needs to take the initiative for harnessing and developing this technology in-house or through means that would be described shortly. The fields that are likely to see this intense rivalry, competition and non-proliferation regimes are nanotechnology and that using rare earth elements. The reason for this is now described below.

Nanotechnology (NT) is a futuristic technology that has already started seeing many applications in the military and civil fields. Working on a billionth of a metre scale (10^{-9} metre) amounts to working with matter on the atomic and molecular levels. This leads to completely different treatment of matter characteristics and drastic miniaturisation of components, stronger but much lighter materials and increased speed of operations in information sharing. It holds immense potential in solar and fuel cells and long life battery technologies – all of these hold immense promise in the field of alternate energy sources. NT has serious military applications too, in allowing greatly improved conventional weapons (allowing better mixing of fuel and oxidiser in energetic composites), miniaturised combat systems and sensors and robots with Artificial Intelligence (AI). The carbon nano-tube, discovered in 1991, has seen a spurt of R&D efforts to find many applications. This is because its tensile strength is 100 fold higher than that of steel while its density is 1/6th that of steel. It has a record strength-density ratio.[4] Its usage, in badminton racquets as carbon composites to scanning probe microscopes and many other applications holds great promise for the future.

As per a study published[5], India ranks 14th in the share of NT publications in the period 1997-99 in a list of 15 countries, but in NT patents, it does not find a place in the top 15 countries. This does not augur well as this technology is now being considered cutting-edge in both the civil and military domains. In the future, NT would be equated to technology associated with weapons of mass destruction due to its immense usage in 'unethical' military applications in biological and chemical warfare and would face commensurate denial regimes. It is paramount that India be involved in developing and procuring NT through the joint development route. The Western countries (especially the USA) have about 20 years headstart in the development of NT with their R&D budgets in the hundreds of millions[6]. It is obvious that NT has dual use application – it would be available for civil as well as military end use. The R&D efforts would also be, thus, carried out by the military and civil organisations. Since its usage for green and medical technology would make it economically very attractive, this would provide yet another reason for limiting its proliferation by the countries that possess the technology. Technology transfer for such technology would almost certainly be restricted and, if permitted, would be prohibitively costly. At this juncture, when the technology is still to mature, the stage is right for India to leverage its economic muscle for joint development and gain a trained pool of scientists and engineers in NT.

The genesis of future conflicts, barring traditional rivalries, would be the intense competition to control and acquire important resources. This competition would start from the point of respective ability to master advanced technology. This technology would allow application and control of natural resources like minerals, water and energy sources. Technology may not be the panacea for wrong political objectives chartering the path of a nation but it would provide synergy to efforts of achieving a dominant position in world affairs. The common index for determining the national efforts of harnessing complex technology is the innovativeness of its people. Innovativeness to use resources is in itself a big plus for a nation on the ascendant trajectory. This brings us to the next issue of control by nations of naturally occurring Rare Earth Elements (REE) and their applications. This precious resource has wide usage in applications in the green and military fields.

REEs are a group of 17 chemical elements. The group consists of yttrium and 15 lanthanide elements (lanthanum, cerium, praseodymium, neodymium, promethium, samarium, europium, gadolinium, terbium, dysprosium, holmium, erbium, thulium, ytterbium, and lutetium). Scandium is found in most rare earth element deposits and is also classified as an REE.[7] These elements have wide usage in the fields of automobiles, petroleum refining, electronics, information technology and rechargeable batteries for vehicles and other applications like cell phones and cameras. With the increase in the demand for green electric vehicles, the demand for these elements is expected to soar. These are also used for air pollution control applications. As mentioned earlier, there is a confluence of green and futuristic military technologies. Applications of REEs are no different. In the defence applications, REEs are also being used for critical futuristic applications. There are many applications that are already in use while many are still in the process of development. Please consider Table 6.1 below:

Table 6.1[8]

Defence Uses of Rare Earth Elements	
Lanthanum	Night-vision goggles
Neodymium	Laser range-finders, guidance systems, communications
Europium	Fluorescents and phosphors in lamps and monitors
Erbium	Amplifiers in fibre-optic data transmission
Samarium	Permanent magnets that are stable at high temperatures
	Precision-guided weapons
	"White noise" production in stealth technology

These metals are difficult to mine even though some of them are found in more abundance than lead, silver and gold. Their discovered mine-able concentrations are less common than for most other ores. The countries that possess large reserves of REEs are China (which contributed to more than 95 percent of the global production in 2010 and has the largest reserves too), the US, Australia, Brazil, India, Malaysia, etc[9]. China has announced that it would drastically reduce its REE exports to ensure supply for indigenous manufacturing. China is probably interested to sell these after value addition for obvious economic reasons. Since India possesses about 3 percent of the total world reserves of REEs, it should strive to develop the technologies based on this resource for its own consumption in military and civil applications. A strategic move would be to gain access to these elements in other countries for long-term requirements. The technologies using REEs in the civil side are mostly commercially available. It is the manufacturing infrastructure for making these products that needs to be set up to cater to the needs of this market, which would only expand. The military applications present a different challenge altogether. Their present and future military applications present an opportunity whose path passes through mastering the civil (and green) applications. Since the basic usage of REEs is based on their almost similar chemical properties, bridging the civil and military applications would be simpler comparatively (with NT); the start is, thus, very important.

...Leading to Technology Transfer

What is technology transfer? This question in its basic form implies transferring the technical know-how from one entity to another. It could be from one country to another or just simply from one organisation to another. The technical know-how could be in the form of (a) imparting knowledge of the manufacturing process; and/or (b) imparting knowledge of maintaining the product after training to assemble it in-house; (c) imparting knowledge of how and why the product was designed in a particular fashion and how to manufacture it in terms of tooling and machinery; (d) co-developing a product so that the basic thought process and knowledge iterations are gone through jointly. In the last case, the entity with a weaker knowledge base leapfrogs many technological gaps that would have been a hindrance in the unilateral development of the product and which would have made it time consuming as well as economically unviable. So, obviously, the entity opting for co-development pays for being a partner as well as shares the economic burden of R&D. The amount of technical knowledge that gets transferred in the first three cases is subjective. It depends upon the complexity of the technology that is required to be mastered. In fact, in a few cases, a prolonged period of executing (a) and (b) together may lead to developing an actual technology base by the recipient entity. It is also dependent upon the existing R&D base of the recipient entity that allows it to absorb the technology associated with a manufacturing process. If the

R&D base is not robust enough, it would become increasingly difficult for the recipient to assimilate the nuances associated with the technology being sought to be adopted and adaptation to the higher technology would become difficult, leading to breakdowns and accidents.

There is another way by which technology transfer is possible but it is not very common. This mechanism entails buying out an organisation that uses an advanced technology and then downward integrating it with one's own set-up in a manner that leads to transfer of know-how. For example, the Tatas bought the Jaguar and Land Rover car companies. If they manage to integrate some nuances of higher end technology being used in these automobiles in their products in India, this integration would lead to an actual transfer of technical know-how. The transfer can take place by either moving the human resource from one location to another or by training on the job, with replication at a home location.

The mechanisms adopted for the transfer are different depending upon the complexity and depth of technology being transferred. This would be explained shortly in the context of the Indian military. The technology asymmetry comes to the fore due to the needs of the recipient and lack of investment in the R&D of the technology at the right time. Sometimes, the recipient entity finds it more economical to invest in the finished product rather than in the R&D process, which may be time and resource consuming. It is also possible that the entity did not possess the strategic fortitude to actually prioritise investment in the development of the particular technology even after possessing the resource for doing the same. To an extent, reverse engineering of a product can also be termed as a mechanism of ToT. This may not be the formal way of ToT but a few countries like China have made handsome gains by following this route. Reverse engineering falls outside the scope of traditional R&D activity if it is carried out to develop the same product. Only if it leads to better understanding as to how and what technology was used to manufacture a particular product, thereby leading to different products, can it be termed as an R&D activity leading to technology development.

It should be clarified here that the author firmly believes that for any ToT to be successful, it is imperative that the human resources of the recipient entity should be made conversant with the new technology development process. Readiness of the human resources to absorb the technology is only possible if the infrastructure to prepare them for it has been readied in advance. For example, if the higher education institutes of a country do not treat R&D as one of their prime objectives, the human resource would never achieve the desired standards for absorbing complex technology; their thought process would not be ready to look beyond the horizon. So even while it is desirable to be involved in the technology development process, the knowledge base of the human resource should be of the desired standards to contribute and also absorb the process. In any other form of ToT (other than both entities being involved in the development process), the complexity of technology may itself lend to the failure of actual transfer if only one of its facets is sought to be transferred. For example, if only production technology of a new product has been transferred, it would be very difficult for the design know-how of the same to be mastered by the recipient entity. This aspect is very important in the context of complex confluence, futuristic technology.

ToT for the Indian Military

India has always strived for achieving self-reliance in military technology for obvious strategic reasons. However, even now, a vast majority of its new military hardware is imported; this speaks volumes about how these attempts have not yielded the desired results. There are many systemic shortcomings but it begins with how the establishment perceives the whole gamut of ToT as a part of India's position in the global geo-politics. The technology denial regime, which would be elaborated upon shortly, has indeed impacted India's quest for higher technology but even now the policies that are being envisaged do not really address the problem in its entirety. On a promising note, it has probably been realised that mistakes have been made and corrective actions are now being put in place by entering into joint ventures in R&D of high end technology. However, this step just about covers one aspect of the problem. R&D of any form, especially in resource efficient technologies, is still not a priority in India. The Ministry of Defence's Defence R&D organisation, which oversees nearly 50 research labs, has remained consistent at about 6 percent of the MoD's budget from 2001 to 2011. In actual terms, the defence spending has grown by 64 percent from 2001 (to 2011) but as a percentage of GDP, it has remained between 2 percent to 3 percent.[10] These figures point towards no great interest in shoring up the R&D structure in India and compare badly with what countries like the US and the UK have been doing. It is no wonder that India continues to rely on technology imports from the developed countries.

New weapons technology development is increasingly based on commercially developed civilian technology. In most developed countries, the defence R&D is driving the civilian technology. In India, the Defence Research and Development Organisation (DRDO) is the only organisation that undertakes defence R&D with almost no forays by the industry. This has forced the DRDO to concentrate on every aspect of military technology, quite a lot of which could have been undertaken by the industry – private or public sector. This affects the required focus towards fundamental research, with seats of higher education not involved in R&D ventures due to lack of partnership (and, thus, funding) opportunity from the industry. The lack of technology development opportunities in India has forced the military establishment to rely more and more on imported technology and superior hardware for maintaining an edge over its adversary. India did try to extract some advantage from this process by resorting to ToT so as to leapfrog the technology race. The process has not been very successful.

The process of ToT followed historically by the Indian military is mentioned in the Indian Defence Procurement Procedure. It envisages four phases of ToT, which leaves a huge question mark over the long-term strategy of the Indian defence forces. These phases cover "fully assembled and tested products" to Semi-Knocked Down (SKD) kits to Completely Knocked Down (CKD) kits to Indigenous Manufacture (IM) kits. Technology transfer followed by the Indian military has been largely restricted to the manufacturing, assemblage and production stages. The SKD phase is the one in which the final assembly and testing of the product is carried out by the Indian production agency; the CKD phase is characterised by the provision of "unassembled Bill of Materials" by the Original Equipment Manufacturer (OEM); Phase-3 (IM kit) is the one in which only the raw materials and components are provided by the OEM and the rest of the task is accomplished by the production agency.[11] What this essentially means is that the production agency would always be dependent on the OEM for raw materials as the rationale behind choosing a particular material would not be understood by the production agency. The OEMs tend to rationalise that the production agency should be able to comprehend the nitty-gritty of each sub-system, assembly, sub-assembly, module, etc after using the product for some time. In India's case, the transition has taken far too much time and is probably still not successful. In such a scenario, the capability for the Indian agencies to be able to transcend the technology being acquired and design hardware from scratch, one with better or even equivalent capability (than that acquired) is difficult and has not happened.

The designing capabilities have not been acquired by the Indian military; even if they have been, the progress has been glacial. Take the case of the HAL Tejas, which is a fourth generation aircraft and is expected to replace the ageing MiG-21 fighters – it is behind schedule. It was supposed to get the Final Operational Clearance (FOC) by 2006. Due to various reasons, including the sanctions imposed after the Pokhran II nuclear tests that blocked the development and delivery of certain key components, its induction got delayed. Finally, the tests were conducted in January 2011 and it is expected to be fully operational only by the end of 2013. The design and development began way back in the 1980s and the Aeronautical Development Agency (ADA) and the Hindustan Aeronautics Limited (HAL) have struggled their way through the process to produce India's first indigenous aircraft. The Sukhoi Su-30 MKI, which the Indian Air Force acquired from Russia, is also a fourth generation aircraft and HAL has been able to produce it although at quite a steep price as all the equipment is provided by the OEM. Yet the Indian agencies have not been able to acquire the state-of-the-art design capabilities. Another example is the Intermediate Jet Trainer (IJT); it took nearly fifteen years to give the Initial Operational Clearance (IOC) to it and it has still not been inducted into the IAF[12]. This despite that fact that the technology involved in a jet trainer is not as complex as that of a full-fledged combat fighter aircraft.

The ToT can be considered a success only if the recipient entity can produce the same product or one which is slightly superior to it at a quick pace. Through reverse engineering, China has been able to do it. India has been lagging behind. The reasons for the time lag could be lack of skilled human resources or technical know-how even though the technology transfer is said to be complete. However, one of the reasons is the lack of coordination between different agencies. It is HAL that is at the receiving end of the ToT (which does not include the design phase technology) but the designing stage is controlled by the ADA. In such a case, even if there is coordination between the two entities, the time taken for the back transition from the production to the design stage could be longer than warranted.

India has perhaps learnt from its experience in shortcomings on ToT and is now on the path of co-development with countries such as Russia. The Sukhoi/HAL Fifth Generation Fighter Aircraft (FGFA) is being developed jointly by India and Russia. This contract was signed in 2010. There is yet another project – the BrahMos programme – for designing, producing and marketing supersonic stealth cruise missiles. The BrahMos Aerospace Joint Venture which came into existence in 1998 involves the DRDO and the Russian NPO Mashinostroyenia, and has been a huge success. The positive results of this enterprise have induced the two countries to move on to new strategic ballistic and cruise missiles.[13] The advantage of joint projects is that these are based on risk-sharing partnerships. The time is ripe for joint ventures between the advanced nations and countries such as India which have enough financial resources to invest by now. Also, the economic recession that has hit the West could force these countries to increasingly invest in joint ventures rather than unilateral ones in which the probability of risk is higher and the future market uncertain.

The future of all machinery – military or otherwise – would be resource efficient technologies. In that sense, the difference between green and military or for that matter, any commercial product would become narrower in the future. The technologies that would go to design and manufacture these efficient and sustainable products would then face obstruction to flow across national boundaries for economic and strategic security reasons. A study of the historical technology denial (or control) regimes for the military and now similar regimes for green technology is mandatory to understand how India can adapt, on its path to self-reliance.

Global Strategy to Control Technology

Technology control and technology denial have become synonymous in the way they are being administered globally. The genesis of technology control can be traced back to the nuclear Non-Proliferation Treaty (NPT). It was meant to deny advanced 'nuclear grade' technology to the countries that had not signed the NPT as well as those that were actually outside the sphere of influence and could be considered as anti-West. The reasons were many – security being the foremost but continued economic dependency was always in the background. Nothing much has changed in the Indian context except that India has signed a special 'nuclear' deal with the US. It had hoped to be given a special entry into the informal 35 (approximately) nation group that at present controls high end, military and dual use technology. This has not happened and, as Brahma Chellaney wrote, "The Americans have committed themselves only to a step-by-step easing commensurate with further Indian actions and concessions."[14] So who finally has the last word on controlling high end technology amongst nations? The US for quite some time (and to an extent even now) had the last word on controlling or denying these technologies to a nation outside their group. The US and its allies have created the following control regimes for this purpose:

- Nuclear Weapons – Nuclear Suppliers Group (NSG).
- Missiles: Missile Technology Control Regime (MTCR).
- Dual Use Technology and Conventional Weapons: The Wassenaar Arrangement.
- Chemical and Biological Weapons: Australia Group.

The control and denial included know-how associated with design and development, production and testing, and material science involved with a particular product or technology. Most of these technologies were/are dual use technologies and have both security as well as commercial exploitation potential. Therefore, in the garb of non-proliferation of security related technologies, the larger aim was also to ensure that the recipient country would not be able to offer competition through cheaper substitute products or services. All these groups were informal arrangements or groupings with no formal body sanction. As per the Wassenaar Arrangement, a common list has been agreed upon by the participating countries, whereby if one country denies such exports, the others would abide by the same. The list is quite exhaustive and varies from high-speed computers, cryogenic equipment to electronic equipment, biotechnology and a range of chemicals. The World Trade Organisation (WTO) does not have a say in this as it has to accept all blanket bans in the name of national security. This effectively ends all debate about the sanctity of the denial regimes.

The question of control regimes encompassing green technology should be on a different page owing to its global good appeal. However, this is not so. Green Technology (GT) like nanotechnology and rare earth products, as already explained, has many dual use appeals and, thus, squarely falls victim to these denial regimes. Yet another challenge to GT Transfer (GTT) is the issue of IPR related economics that has posed hurdles to the process. Thus, GTT would face twin hurdles in technology transfer and these aspects would be covered separately. This confluence of economic and strategic use is the bane of technology transfers in almost all sectors. This is explained in detail in the succeeding paragraphs.

GT is being touted as a strategically very important asset for any nation state. This is mainly due to two reasons. There is increasing pressure on countries to switch to green technology for meeting energy requirements as the perils of environmental change and exploding world population are increasingly being felt across the globe. Secondly, the line between green and commercial (even military) technology is very thin as the desired end use remains the same – resource and energy efficiency. GTT has been envisaged in all the documents and declarations of the climate change negotiations since the 1992 Earth Summit. Under this, the developed countries (mostly belonging to the Annex-I category created under the UNFCCC) are expected to transfer both technological as well as financial resources to the developing countries to cope with climate change in terms of both adaptation and mitigation. ToT was discussed at Copenhagen and Cancun, and agreements were arrived to encourage ToT and the foundation for the technology mechanism was laid. The Durban Conference (2011) also stressed on the importance of ToT and in this respect, the establishment of the technology mechanism consisting of a Technology Executive Committee and a Climate Technology Centre and Network has been envisaged. This mechanism was recommended by the international community in order to ensure that lack of information or training in some of the Least Developed Countries (LDCs) would not hinder innovation and development of technologies in these countries.

Movement of technologies from the developed to the developing countries has been obstructed by the former for a long time for various reasons, including the fear of losing a competitive edge in the technological market on account of reproduction of technologies by the recipient countries. As already mentioned, one of the biggest hindrances to ToT has been identified as IPR. The patent law forms a part of the Trade Related Aspects of Intellectual Property Rights (TRIPS) agreements of 1994 that were adopted under the WTO. Whether it is the adaptation technologies that help countries to adapt to the vagaries of climate change or the conversion technologies that assist countries to reduce the impact of human activities on the environment such as reducing carbon emissions, the main challenge is to make sure that these technologies are accessible to the developing countries. The patent law could be called successful only if it promotes innovation. Between 2000 and 2009, patent applications associated with solar energy production multiplied by three (85 applications in 2009), those linked to wind or hydraulic energy by four (42 and 43 applications respectively in 2009), and those linked to alternative propulsion systems for means of transport by 2.5 (125 patents in 2009).[15] The fact that the intellectual property matters are dealt with by the WTO while everything else related to the environment is being discussed under the auspices of the UN has made ToT highly difficult. The Copenhagen, Cancun and Durban Summits failed to resolve the issue of IPR since the developed countries insisted on not discussing it under the aegis of the UNFCCC as it was already part of the WTO agenda. The developed countries have refused to agree to relaxation of the patent law as, according to them, such a move would hamper research and innovation. Data reveals that ten leading patent holders in green technologies are the Organisation for Economic Cooperation and Development (OECD) countries; the only exception is China that is ranked fourth currently[16]. Developing countries have been insisting that just as there are exceptions in the case of pharmaceuticals and medical treatments as every WTO member has the right to protect public health, there should be similar provisions in the case of green technologies too. How far the IPR regime can be bypassed, is a moot point since innovations demand investment in R&D and without expecting a return, it is not right to expect investment. The suggestion by the developing countries now is more nuanced and focussed on providing a financial mechanism to overcome the IPR barrier.

Another type of technology growth barrier now being seen is the rigorous control of natural resources. China's control of exports of rare earth elements is a strategy towards this end with a view to control the world market of its finished products. This has another potential of suppressing the development of rare earth based applications for military use. This is where India can fall in a technology suppression trap if it does not enter the technology development cycle now. Its scientists have to be exposed to the applications of these technologies so that they are ready to expand their usage in related fields without having to rely on a few favourable countries in the future. Relying on a nuclear deal like package in the future is fraught with inherent danger. Even in this, the US has offered no commitment, let alone a timetable, to lift technology controls. It has only "committed to a strengthened and expanded dialogue on export-control issues through fora such as the US-India High Technology Cooperation Group (HTCG)". HTCG was formed in 2003, with a mandate to ensure that the US exports in a few specific areas pick up. These areas included nanotechnology amongst others like water treatment and defence and strategic trade, etc.[17] It is clear that the Indian model of technology transfer in the military technology has to evolve, to lead to the much desired aim of self-reliance. Similarly, the IPR issue currently plaguing the green technology negotiations can be resolved with commitments from the developed countries and transparency in bilateral relations, which is actually easier said than done. However, a model is being suggested for green technology too so that while respecting the IPR rights of entities, a way forward can be achieved.

The Way Forward

The US Air Force in 1946 contracted with the Douglas Aircraft Company of Santa Monica, California, for Project RAND (Research and Development). Initially intended to provide advice on certain technical problems, it expanded to become an independent non-profit corporation with civilian experts assuming roles in strategic planning, economics, political scientists and engineers, etc. It remains one of the biggest and most active think-tanks in the US, concentrating on many socially relevant matters, including military strategy[18]. This is a prime example of strategic thinking without which innovations would be difficult to come by. While a technical think-tank in the US goes on to become an all encompassing centre that is globally held in high esteem, the Indian policy-makers should be suitably motivated to form and utilise such centres of excellence within the country. Strategic thinking on the subject is a must and the exposure of the young bureaucracy at an early stage to such a thought process would reap handsome dividends. There is no loss of face in working with think-tanks that can do focussed conceptual level work, something that is not always possible within the four walls of a government office where dousing the day-to-day fire is the primary task. Only with such thinking can long-term national growth and development strategies be put in place.

The Western militaries realised the importance of training their soldiers in military science and engineering so that they could customise innovations for military use. George Owen Squier (1865-1934) was the US Army's first Ph.D. Forty years of electrical research won him many radio patents. He founded the army's first signals school at Fort Leavenworth, Kansas, and later, the army's radio research laboratory. He also pioneered army aviation.[19] Swiss Majors Bode and Rubin were instrumental in innovating the first successful metal-jacketed bullet in the early 1880s.[20] The US military now has the Office of Naval Research (ONR), the Army Research Office and Air Force Office of Scientific Research. The ONR also serves as a training ground for science administrators throughout the government.[21] The Indian defence establishment has the Defence Research and Development Organisation (DRDO) for defence related R&D. It would be worthwhile to compare the efficacy of the individual

Services research wings/organisations with a healthy mix of serving defence personnel and civilian scientists vis-à-vis the existing set-up of DRDO as a separate study. The oft-cited communication gap between the Services and DRDO as being the bane of technology development in India and lack of indigenous project fructification, may then become a thing of the past.

For self-reliance in critical military or dual use technology, overall R&D efforts have to be inclusive of the industry's efforts with enhanced funding. A major lacuna in Indian self-reliance forays has been a lack of clear focus on developing an R&D base within the country. Even when these shortcomings were realised, the approach, as outlined in the Defence Procurement Procedures was not comprehensive. India's total spending on R&D (as per data of December 2010) was about one percent of its GDP as compared to the US and Japan which spend about 3 to 3.5 percent of their GDP.[22] The number of scientists and engineers as a ratio of the population is one of the lowest in India. So what exactly is the panacea for reversing this process? There is no one cure and as the failure is systemic, the solutions have to be aimed at the same level.

First and foremost, the R&D spending in India has to be drastically enhanced. Involvement of private industry in the process is very important because only then one can see concerted efforts at commercialisation of technology, which is essential to ensure further innovations. The focus of the research efforts has to be in confluence technology. Since India has lagged behind in the race for developing these technologies for large scale commercial application, the best course of action would be to go in for joint ventures in R&D with other developed countries; considering the present global economic scenario, they would be interested in funding sources that India can bring to the table. This approach would help bridge the gaps that are being faced by the Indian scientists in developing the applications of dual use technologies. It would also ensure that India does not have to go in for purchases of different products belonging to the same generic technology, separately and at great cost. The barriers to technology would then not have to be faced for each product. Once the generic technology is mastered, joint product development would ensure a newer geo-political alignment emerging of which India would be a strategic partner, free to use the technology anyway it wants to, for its development.

Only large spending and joint R&D would not ensure mastering the confluence technologies of the future. The human resource has to be adequately ready for absorbing the technology. This issue is well understood internationally even for GTT, as mentioned earlier in the context of the least developed countries. For mastering the cutting edge technology for military applications, it is essential that the best brains are tapped at a stage that is free of life's encumbrances. India's premier engineering and science institutes produce engineers and scientists who go abroad and do path-breaking work. It is obvious that they possess the potential but that remains untapped by our R&D establishment. There is hardly any connectivity between the industry/ government research labs and the best engineering colleges. The project-funding based approach is not followed up with them, thus, never exposing these students to anything more than the theoretical knowledge in the books. If the Indian industry then laments that these students do not possess the requisite expertise that can be readily absorbed by them in their labs, the onus lies squarely on them too. Preparing the student engineers and scientists has to begin early for more application based study as different from a pure theoretical knowledge base. This is applicable to all branches of engineering and pure sciences with the probable exception of information technology.

Another step towards self-reliance is the strong drivers for patents. The Indian policy-makers have long believed that an institute's or a lab's worth is measured by the number of papers it manages to publish in scientific journals – national and international. This is a very important step in the process of technology development but only a STEP! Until it culminates in a patent product, the work is not complete. There would be many scientists who would cry foul at the advocacy for patents as their basic aim is to develop the science and not its applications. It is not meant to belittle their contribution; it is rather to point out the inadequacy of the process that does not take this step towards its logical contribution. Probably a team approach to developing a patent might be essential. The team may consist of engineers and scientists, thus, ensuring fructification of the research into an actual development of a product or process. Only with such an approach can the industry be involved, bringing about an infusion of funds into R&D activity, leading to its exponential growth. A commercial exploitation of futuristic technology should be the desired result of any R&D effort. It would be too much to expect that all research attempts lead to patents but when this is considered the desirable outcome by the Indian establishment, the results would be commensurate. Consider the excerpts of a news article in the box below, which speaks volumes about how the policy-makers at the top level are concerned about these issues.

Box 1[23]

The 'China vs India' debate saw Prime Minister Manmohan Singh noting that India's "relative position in the world of science is declining, and the nation has been overtaken by countries like China".

Speaking at the 99th Indian National Science Congress on Tuesday, the PM's inaugural lecture, meant to celebrate scientific advances in India, was tempered with some hard facts and hints of why research in the country is lagging.

"As far as resources are concerned, the fraction of GDP spent on R&D in India has been too low and stagnant. We must aim to increase the total R&D spending as a percentage of GDP to 2 percent by the end of the 12th Plan Period from the current level of about 0.9 percent," the Prime Minister said.

He accepted that the private sector is contributing one-fourth of research. But his suggestion that this has to increase further was in part an indictment of public sector research centres.

"It is in some ways ironic that GE and Motorola have created world class technology hubs in India, while our own industry has not done so, except perhaps in the pharma sector," the PM added in a criticism of the science policy as well as domestic industrial giants.

While Singh did reaffirm that "India had moved from the 15th rank in 2003 to 9th position in 2010 with respect to the number of publications in peer valued journals", he also pointed out that India lagged behind in applied sciences and the focus was fixed more on fundamental research.

Union Science and Technology and Earth Sciences Minister Vilasrao Deshmukh, too, made a comparison with China, claiming India was lagging on applied sciences. "China publishes five times more patents than India," he said.

The PM also reflected on how students of sciences shifted to other careers after education. "While it is true that science and engineering continue to attract the best students, many of them later opt for other careers because of poor prospects in science."

It is obvious that the policy-makers are concerned but are they doing enough or is it that democracy has forced India's hand towards being a more socialist state at the cost of future development? The 2 percent of GDP investment in R&D, which has been spoken of by the PM is a very conservative figure in real terms and does not match up to other countries that have a headstart in technology development. This growth is being targeted only by 2017. A better strategy would be the co-development process that has been outlined earlier and this should be targeted by India to fast track the R&D efforts in India.

Till the R&D process is fast tracked, India has to make itself a manufacturing hub if it wants to enjoy the real benefits of ToT rather than questioning the denial and IPR regimes. The same regimes could even profit the Indian entities – both public and private – if they come up with high-tech designs through the in-house development process. China has been able to excel in this endeavour, evidenced by the manner in which it has exploited its rare earth reserves. India could be a cheaper manufacturing base than China and much more accessible. The investment polices (read taxation and licence regimes) in India would need to be better tuned to attract the high end technology products, especially ones made by dual use technology. A special dispensation for attracting green/energy efficient/renewal energy generation and confluence technology and manufacturing applications, is needed. A separate initiative is required for overcoming the IPR barrier discussed earlier.

Overcoming IPR Controls

Just as public health has been exempted from the IPR regime, the Indian stand has been that the law should be relaxed for green technology as well depending on the needs of the developing countries and the terms agreeable to the patent holding entity. This stand is obviously desirable, considering the 'historical responsibility' of the developed countries in perpetuating the environment change. However, it does not take into account the business end model of the transaction, which is important if IPR controls are to be overcome. Without working out the economics of innovation, it would be expecting too much from the recession hit economies to part with technology just for the global good. Moreover, being a country that is developing at a fast pace, India is not expected to be given such concessions at this stage. Even a country such as China that has stood by most of the principles raised by India at the negotiations, does not support India on the IPR issue, primarily because China sees itself as a major technology vendor in the future, with its mammoth investment in green technologies in the past few years. With no international support for India's proposals, the policy-makers should now change their stand and look at alternatives rather than harping on propositions that are doomed to failure.

A broad international agreement can be worked out that would allow any two countries to enter into bilateral agreements by which technology could be transferred from one country to another. There could be GTT from a private entity or from a government one to another country. In the case of the patent being held by a government entity, it has to quantify the IPR and fix the price of the technology being transferred. It could do this by demanding limited royalties or no royalties at all from the recipient entity. The project could be registered with the technology mechanism so that it could be endorsed by the UN. The monetary contribution by the developed country i.e. the royalty forgone by it in the transfer process and as accepted by the centralised UN mechanism funds, could then be counted as its contribution to the envisaged Green Fund (GF), to which the developed countries have already pledged to contribute. This is the reason why there has to be close coordination between the technological mechanism and the financial mechanism. Similarly, if the patent holder is a private entity, the government of the country to which this entity belongs would have to first finalise all the provisions with it and pay the royalties (if any) to it and, at the same time, register it under the technology mechanism and this would be deemed as a contribution to the GF of an equivalent amount that it uses to buy the patent or pay the royalty. This is a simple solution that is fraught with the risk of manipulation by the developed countries during the technology pricing determination. However, this can be overcome by ensuing that cartelisation of a particular technology is not permitted and the recipient country is permitted to approach any developed country having a particular technology to seek transfer and decide on the pricing in a bilateral manner before the transaction is put up to the UN technology mechanism. All technology denial groupings that have been mentioned earlier would have to pledge that they would not block GTT even if the technology has some dual use. This agreement would have to be brokered through the UNFCCC and not under the WTO, and has pros and cons for both sides – the haves and have nots of technology. In this way, the hurdles of the IPR regime could be overcome and, at the same time, innovation would not be blocked.

Some of the ways in which technology transfer can be made more efficient and even-handed are as follows:

- Not only should the decision-making bodies of the UN comprise countries from both the developed and the developing/underdeveloped blocs but also it should operate on equal terms and not on the basis of financial contribution.
- Technology cooperation should be given a boost apart from technology transfer so that the relatively financially well-off developing countries need not depend on the developed countries for the latest technologies besides the fact that the equations of competitive advantage would serve both blocs' interests.
- The needs of different countries could be different and, therefore, an appropriate analysis of the needs has to be done before the deployment of technology.
- Autonomous scientific appraisal, public-private partnerships in technology development, involvement of the Non-Governmental Organisation (NGOs) and civil society in the implementation of the projects as well as establishment of a feedback system are essential.

Balancing an Imperfect World

Technology transfer would lead to greater balance in the world militarily and economically; technology and technical innovations are inextricably linked with development and their absence has the potential to exacerbate class differences amongst nations.. However, it is to be understood that technological sophistication can provide a military edge over an adversary in a battle but is not sufficient for winning a war. This fact was amply proven in the US-Vietnam War. Tactical and organisational strategic ideas are required to convert technology into winning applications; technology development for the sake of achieving scientific research milestones does not always lead to superiority of a military product that can be used for achieving war aims. In the same context, confluence technologies, till they are resource efficient, would continue to provide an edge to the entity controlling them and, thus, attempts to master them would be blocked by the entities that control them. Technology transfer can fill a void but the path forward is to effectively develop futuristic technologies in-house and then control their applications. For this, the R&D in the field of science and its application have to come of age in the country. The systemic gaps thwarting these undertakings have to be removed.

It cannot be denied that "acceptance" and "cultural assimilation" as well as "combining of technological and cultural paradigms" are requirements for "successful technology transfer."[24] Culture is very closely connected to technology transfer. Very often, the cultural transfer is considered a pre-requisite for technological transfer. Technological practice is an integral part of any nation's culture and this is shaped by the requirements of that nation in terms of its security and its resources. Some of the technologies may not be a necessity for every country. For example, the requirements of India are completely different from those of the Maldives. Similarly, the foreign technologies have to be absorbed by the recipient country by not only building mechanisms that would facilitate the physical transfer but also the psychological, cultural and technical transfer. India has been lagging in the latter, especially in imbibing the technological practices of the industrialised countries.

The interaction between the industry and R&D is very low in India. We access technologies from other countries at great costs and these are not always first rate. In the US, Nobel Laureates run their own businesses. We do not have one such example in our country. The disconnect between different domains has to be bridged – education and its application, industry and educators; these disconnects have ensured that India does not rank anywhere in the top countries in the field of innovation even if there are many excellent seats of higher education. The seats of higher education and the industry have to synergise their efforts towards achieving the objectives of application based research. A business model has to become effective for harnessing the talent of these educational institutes.

The technology transfer barriers are here to stay. Overtly, they have a security related rationale but the economic agenda is always in the background. Emerging economies like India would, thus, always face this hurdle in the quest for a more dominant position in global affairs. Therefore, it is essential that cutting edge work in futuristic technologies like nanotechnology and those using rare earth elements is started in right earnest. The technologies of tomorrow would be resource efficient and, thus green, as resources, especially, natural resources would be hard to obtain. Thus, there would be a confluence of technologies used in green applications, in military and normal commercial applications. And, with mastery of these technologies, a nation would be able to take strategic decisions independently, without any pressure. It is not a desirable situation if India is relegated to a lower position, globally, in the indices of technology and patents. India has to start assuming the role of an emerging power.

Notes

1. Doubleday Canada, a division of Random House of Canada Limited 2006, p.60.
2. http://ideas.repec.org/a/aen/journl/1992v13-04-a07.html, accessed on December 21, 2011. These postulates suggest that with increase in efficiency, the resource consumption increases.
3. T.W. Lee, *Military Technologies of the World – Vol II* (Westport USA: Praeger Security International, 2009), p. 364.
4. Jurgen Altmann, *Military Nanotechnology* (UK: Routledge Oxon, 2006), p. 23.
5. Ibid., p. 36.
6. Ibid., p. 39, pp 63-68.
7. http://geology.com/articles/rare-earth-elements/accessed on December 29, 2011.
8. Ibid.
9. For exact figures, please refer to the website at Ibid.
10. For more information, please visit http://casi.ssc.upenn.edu/system/files/RR+ +CSIS.pdf, accessed on January 3, 2012.
11. For more information, see "Defence Procurement Procedure – 2011," Ministry of Defence, Government of India, http://mod.nic.in/dpm/DPP2011.pdf, accessed on December 30, 2011.
12. "Indigenous Jet Trainer to get Initial Clearance by July," *India Strategic*, February

2011, see http://www.indiastrategic.in/topstories906.htm, accessed on December 29, 2011.

13. Konstantin Makiyenko, "BrahMos Sets the 'Gold Standard for Russian-Indian Defence Projects," *Russia and India Report*, August 22, 2011, see http://indrus.in/articles/2011/08/22/brahmos_sets_the_gold_standard_for_russian-indian_defence_projects_12899.html, accessed on December 30, 2011.
14. http://www.livemint.com/2010/11/15200220/Controlling-technology-flows.html, accessed on January 2, 2012.
15. Guillaume Henry, "Intellectual Property Rights and Green Technologies," 42nd World Congress of the International Association for the Protection of Intellectual Property, 2010, p. 9, see http://www.aippi.fr/upload/Prix%20AIPPI/greentech-ipr-1st-academic-prize-dr.-guillaume-henry.pdf, accessed on December 30, 2011.
16. Ibid., p. 26
17. Ibid.
18. For more details, readers may visit the website http://www.rand.org/about/history.html, accessed on December 23, 2011.
19. Barton C. Hacker, with assistance from Margaret Vining, *American Military Technology: The Life Story of a Technology* (Westport, US: Greenwood Press), pp. 39-40.
20. Ibid., p. 41.
21. Ibid., p. 113.
22. For a full report, please refer http://www.battelle.org/aboutus/rd/2011.pdf, accessed on January 3, 2012.
23. Nitin Sethi, "China's Stolen R&D March on India, Says PM," *The Times of India*, Delhi edition, January 4, 2012.
24. Bernhard Irrgang, "Technology Transfer and Modernization: What can Philosophers of Technology Contribute?" *Technology Transfer and Modernization*, December, 2007, p. 5, see http://ubiquity.acm.org/article.cfm?id=1331965, accessed on December 30, 2011.

7

Shrinking the Energy Bubble

I wear a Seiko eco-drive watch. It is a costly watch, not by the standards of 'Rolex' and 'Rado' but by the size of my modest pay-check. The watch does not need a battery to operate and gets charged by body motion. Even moderate body motion suffices for charging it but since I don't have the habit of taking off the watch during my regular gym visits and everyday badminton games, charging it is not a problem. Once charged fully, the watch works accurately for many days without the necessity of being charged. Now don't get me wrong. I am not re-selling the watch! But what the battery-less operation has done is to remove one worry from my mind: knowing that the watch would not turn inaccurate whilst indicating that the battery life is coming to an end, and since I do not own a duplicate watch, to ensure an immediate replacement of the battery. My one time investment has actually paid off albeit the initial higher cost, giving me peace of mind and independence by removing my dependence on back-up resources. This is the essence of operational benefits that any military can accrue while shrinking its energy bubble.

Energy Security for the Military

In February 2012, RAdm Neil Morisetti, the UK's envoy on climate change and energy security, speaking at the Centre for Air Power Studies, New Delhi, on ensuring energy supplies in Afghanistan and Iraq, mentioned the high costs the military has to pay for safeguarding the fuel convoys in a hostile environment. The military commanders there welcomed any move – administrative or technological – to reduce their dependency on fuel. The higher costs in terms of human lives and resources spent actually remove the flexibility in planning operations without any encumbrances. In reality, any military would strive for freedom in planning its operations. While training or in actual hostilities, support resources planning is one of the paramount activities for the military. Energy supply is a vital support resource for undertaking any operation and, therefore, takes very high precedence in the military planning paradigms. A lower reliance on energy would signify greater freedom in planning of operations and may even be the difference between life and death during actual hostilities.

While operational preparedness would remain a top priority with the military leadership, the welcome fallout of reduced dependency on energy would be checking the environmental degradation. In India, the defence sector is not recognised as one that can contribute towards carbon mitigation. So much so that the Ministry of Defence (MoD) is not even a line ministry in the institutional network arrangement for green house gas inventory development, while the second National Communication (NATCOM) to the United Nations Framework Convention for Climate Change (UNFCCC) is being prepared.[1] This does not mean that once it becomes mandatory for India to commit to internationally mandated mitigation targets post 2020 [when the post Kyoto Protocol II period starts and as decided at the Durban Conference of Parties (COP) in 2011], the situation would not change. National legislations in the USA and the European Union (with certain exceptions for the armed forces) mandate that all federal government facilities/departments have to conform to the laid-down environment laws, including energy efficiency and emissions targets.[2]

It is important for the military to understand the interrelation between terms like energy efficiency, conservation and the military's operational readiness. When seen in the context of the national and global commitments for reducing energy intensity as well as environmental impacts of a carbon intensive energy regime, positive actions by the military in this field would amount to a bold leadership decision. While the importance of saving costs due to energy savings makes eminent sense for a commercial organisation, in the tough global economic scenario prevailing presently, this becomes an imperative even for the military. This chapter would not only try to capture the quintessence of energy security from the military's operational perspective but would also concentrate on how it can reduce its energy dependency by showcasing some good practices being followed by other militaries around the globe. While undertaking research prior to writing this book (and specifically for this chapter), it became obvious that most of the examples of environmental consideration in the military are from countries which were legally mandated to reduce carbon emissions as a part of the Kyoto Protocol and not otherwise. This goes on to prove that even now, the military around the globe is a reluctant entrant in the field of environmental leadership.

Energy security has been part of a country's security concerns as without the availability of energy, a country cannot progress. The geo-political, security and strategic considerations are taken into account to ensure energy availability for meeting a country's needs. Almost all countries have, therefore, tried to expand their energy basket to broaden the base of energy procurement with both the types and sources of energy being expanded. In the case of energy security specifically for the military, the issues are similar to what a large manufacturing, power intensive industry would face if its operations are disturbed due to absence of power. It must have back-ups and contingency plans in place to ensure that the impact of non-availability of energy is kept to the minimum. For the military, the stakes involved are much higher. So in addition to ensuring availability of energy for undertaking missions, they would be much better off if they can reduce their dependency on it to whatever extent possible; for the other initiatives, their endeavour should be to become self-sufficient and renewable sources of energy offer them this luxury. In both these ventures, environmental degradation is checked, the country's low carbon trajectory is maintained, and that is a welcome outcome.

Energy security in the context of the military and national priority would imply adequate energy availability at all times as this is the main resource for undertaking allotted/planned tasks, achieving growth and ensuring development. Reliance on hydrocarbons imported from a few countries of the Middle East poses its own set of challenges in terms of cost volatility, maintaining the lines of communication and trade routes. This is primarily a challenge that has both military and political/diplomatic connotations. As the nation enlarges its options of energy resources with a firm focus on non-carbon or less carbon intensive sources, the military also needs to be prepared to reduce consumption and meet its energy requirements efficiently from renewable but reliable sources. The issue of energy security, thus, needs to be tackled at both the fronts simultaneously – increase efficiency of usage and reduce/conserve the total energy being used.

While on a visit to Indonesia as a United Nations Environment Programme (UNEP) resource person to learn and share the good practices in management of Ozone Depleting Substances (ODS),[3] I interacted with their military personnel. The interaction was facilitated by the Indonesian National Ozone Unit. I clarified at the start of the interaction that I was there as a UNEP resource person in my personal capacity and not as a representative of my country's military. Therefore, I was both taken aback and amused when the question of "what have you come here to sell" was posed to me during my interactive presentation, which was surprisingly the first question. It was not easy for the military officers there to appreciate that a serving military officer from India would be interested to talk to them on ODS management and nothing else. By the end of my talk, I had many Indonesian military friends – a few converts and some sceptics who were willing to grant me a point or two. I also realised why the military has not been enthusiastic about taking up environmental matters. This is because a business case has never been made out for them to take the leadership in this field. The cost-benefit analysis is essential to swing the leadership anywhere. The only difference in the case of the military is that cost in its terminology means more than mere money but also human lives and benefit means not only in the balance sheet but also war-fighting capability. In the same context, it has to be convinced that energy is a capability enhancer for the organisation and not merely a part of the social responsibility for safeguarding the environment.

The Mindset Dinosaur

The military has hardly been exposed to energy source pressures. It has existed in its bubble without being unduly bothered by the rising costs of energy, questions of consumption patterns, energy audits and thoughts of adverse impact of higher dependency on energy on its operations. This 'generation gap' has started to narrow down! With the rise in the prices of hydrocarbons and fickleness of supplies from the Middle East, owing to instability of various types, old paradigms are now giving way to a new reality. The military facilities around the globe are turning to become more energy-efficient and revelling in the cost benefits that this has offered. Sharon Burke, as head of a new energy office at the Pentagon, is charged with finding ways for the US armed forces to cut their dangerous reliance on oil. In an interview in December 2010, the cost of energy that is used by the US armed forces is quoted more than once by her.[4] If it has started pinching the largest GDP economy (in gross terms) of the world, how can the weaker or emerging economies afford to ignore it?

A few years ago, while working in a regional HQ of the IAF, I was required to attend a meeting/brain-storming session, ostensibly called to discuss the ways by which the electricity bill of the formation could be made more representative of actual consumption by the sub-formation utilities and office/domestic complexes. The Commander-in-Chief was a concerned man as the total bill was somehow more every year. Most of the military officers assembled, including me, thought this to be a light-hearted exchange of ideas. When the Chairman, a two-star General, briefed us on the problem with sincerity, a few of us came up with copy-book solutions of switching off lights when leaving a room, motion sensors for corridor lighting and educational programmes for families and children (in schools). Predictably, this did not impress the Chairman. He was interested in out of the box solutions. In a moment of hubris, I told the Chairman that if we knew which installations were the causes of the inflated bills, we could attend to them specifically. We were surprised to learn that not all the installations had separate electricity meters and, thus, the problem could not be pinpointed. Now the discussion moved away from the ordinary and went on to explore more systemic changes required for tackling the issue. The traditional mindset was broken and its dinosaur was on its way to becoming extinct. The point that naturally comes to mind is, why was the Commander-in-Chief the only individual who felt it necessary to find a solution to the issue of high electricity usage? Why was the Chairman not satisfied with the mere lip-service that we were paying to the issue? The answers are actually very simple. Only he had seen the costs that were being incurred to sustain the present consumption level. The junior lot of officers (like me) were not much bothered because it did not affect them directly and appreciation of the harmful impact of such actions on the organisation as well as the environment was way beyond the traditional military thinking. This has to change, and more and more commanders are realising that the resources can be much better optimised than they are being at present, provided we are able to break the old thought process. This is only possible if the military hierarchies realise the difference that can be caused by resource conservation actions on the organisational working environment.

There would still be high energy usage in the military as the facilities are largely dependent on the same. It is here that the old and traditional way of thinking of commercial energy availability has taken its toll. The use of diesel generating systems for back up of the primary power source for operational systems has been ingrained in the military working procedures. The military in many countries is still not able to think of energy security from the perspective of its own off-grid production system, something that has become a regular feature in the Western economies. The off-grid production is always from renewable sources like solar or wind even for operational usage. This old mindset has to change to obtain flexibility in options as well as for environmental considerations, which would become mandatory in the near future. Some case studies on the subject would be highlighted later in the chapter. The first step towards incorporating energy efficiency in any organisation would obviously be laying down the targets that these forays should achieve. Setting up targets is more essential in the military as its personnel are not comfortable working with abstract principles.

The Goal

Without a goal to pursue, it would be difficult to really drive any organisation, and military organisations are no different. These goals are articulated by the top management to showcase their own commitment to the cause, which will then motivate the staff placed at lower echelons to actively work towards the target. In the case of the military, the policies on lowering energy dependency should ideally be articulated by the

MoD. It should clearly spell out the desired outcome of energy efficiency and consumption reduction programme that needs to be instituted in the organisation. Specific energy programme implementation policies, strategies to be adopted, and goals would have to be provided in the form of MoD directives to lay down the management responsibilities. Goals should be quantitative and developed through audits as would be explained in the next chapter (Chapter 8) and strategies should include awareness and training programmes, Life Cycle Cost (LCC) methodologies, energy audit procedures, renewable/clean energy programmes, financing mechanisms, and need for energy-efficient buildings. Financing mechanisms for energy conservation have to be built in the overall budgetary allotment,[5] even specifying a well defined procedure for private enterprises to contribute to energy efficiency measures of the military/federal departments. Since management responsibilities are to be defined by the MoD, it is suggested that this should be for the top hierarchy only; the responsibility of percolating these responsibilities into the lower echelons should be assigned to the individual Service Headquarter.

The MoD in India would have to be a lot more proactive in managing the energy efficiency/conservation issues within the military. Since the pursestrings are in its hands, responsible spending also needs to be ensured by it. This brings us to a desired future state for the ministry with respect to energy. It will have to ensure the following few imperatives for a successful energy management programme.

- Establish and monitor a ministry-wide energy inventory.
- Enhance effectiveness of planning by institutionalising energy solutions in the MoD planning and implementation processes.
- Increase energy security for the military through strategic resilience by building reliance on alternative and renewable sources of energy leading to reduced dependence on volatile supplies of oil and leveraging efforts by other organisations like research laboratories, industry and the academia.
- The operational effectiveness has to be enhanced by reducing the military's total energy demands.

Resource Efficiency Begins with Energy Efficiency

India uses much less energy on per capita basis than even smaller countries like Finland but if this mostly comes from polluting sources like coal, with a very low efficiency/conversion rate, the resources utilised even for generating the low amount of energy would be disproportionate to the value redeemed. This situation cries out for a change, and fast. Since the energy sources would predominantly be hydrocarbon-based, reducing their consumption is an imperative to reduce the carbon 'bootprint' of the military.

The term energy efficiency has become ubiquitous in our every day life. It is fashionable as a market gimmick for the sale of products; it appeals to the sensitised generation as it helps in safeguarding the environment; and now it is a requirement for many domestic products/appliances in the Indian market. The biggest barrier to sustainable living happens to be the umbilical cord that connects quality of life with energy usage. So it is automatically construed that higher quality of life and growth, development and prosperity are possible only with the supporting backbone of higher and still higher energy consumption. Calling this connectivity the 'Business as Usual' or BAU model, growth and development have come to be linked with carbon emissions as a consequence of high energy usage. The Western or developed countries followed this path during the industrialisation era, resulting in degradation of the environment. Now the high growth economies of the world like India, China, Brazil, etc. are being implored not to follow suit. The way forward is then following a less energy intensive[6] path. Since 1990, the energy used as a ratio of US$ 1,000 of GDP has decreased by about 10 percent globally, with the transition economies of Eastern and Southern Asia registering the highest gains in efficiency,[7] thus, trying to break the BAU model. However, the energy use can be decreased by using energy efficiently as well as conserving its usage. Efficiency and conservation efforts have to be followed simultaneously; otherwise the desired effect would not be forthcoming. This would be explained in greater detail later. Whether it is electricity or fuel that is used in any organisation, the energy usage has a price tag attached to it. Cost consideration itself, if not environmental concern, should suffice to sustain the drive for energy efficiency and conservation.

As a first step towards resource efficiency, building energy efficiency is usually the low-hanging fruit. Constant evaluation and evolution of equipment and technology to make them more energy efficient is a norm in the corporate world due to obvious cost considerations. A similar culture can be easily instituted in a defence organisation. The considerations would be different for operational and mission critical equipment like military hardware required for combat and training, building utilities – both operational and non-operational equipment like recreational apparatus, transportation and facilities for the troops and their families in the messes, etc. While the energy-efficient military hardware would have to be customised against the specific requirements of the customer (please refer to Chapter 5 on green procurements), non-operational energy-efficient hardware is available off the shelf. With the introduction of energy rating of equipment in India and expansion in its scope, such equipment would be easily available. The military has to ensure that only energy-efficient equipment is preferred in its bulk procurement procedures, which are carried out under the defence and government supplies rate contract. Even for other methods of procurements, energy efficiency should become a desirable feature for all equipment. Active cooperation between the industry and the military is very important. It is meant to ensure introduction of efficient products for both operational and non-operational equipment. Energy efficiency has to become a key performance parameter in the acquisition process, an attribute of a system that is considered critical to the development of its military capability. It is reported[8] that China's People's Liberation Army (PLA) and the armed police forces are working together to construct 100 major **energy-efficient training bases** to be used by the country's 2.3 million Servicemen. The military will be lowering its energy use as part of a **nation-wide emission-reduction plan**, although it may be kept in mind that both China and India are currently not obliged to do so. The Chinese 12th Five-Year Plan specifically states the role of the military in these environment saving measures as, "Efforts to save resources in the military are an important part of the country's energy-saving and emission-reduction efforts." In comparison, the Indian Planning Commission's report[9] on low carbon growth for the Indian economy does not have anything to say for the military. This focus has to be built as the military is a high consumer of energy and has the potential to lower consumption.

Some of the places where energy-efficient products can be easily introduced with synergistic gains are listed below. This list does not contain the energy efficiency norms that can be incorporated in a building as that is a separate subject in itself and a brief introduction to the same would be given later in the chapter. It is to be appreciated that this list cannot be exhaustive and each and every organisation would have to draw its own procedures to evaluate the list of equipment where energy efficiency norms should be a primary criterion of selection. While suggesting this list of equipment, I have deliberately not differentiated between operational or non-operational end-use of the equipment under consideration. This is because energy-efficiency norms are not being recommended as a *quid pro quo* for operational efficiency so as to require a separate rationale for grouping, and also because the standards are applicable across the board.

- Fuel efficient vehicles – both load carriers and staff cars. Introduction of new vehicles should cover this aspect directly and inefficient replacements should be rejected. There is no rationale for introducing later generation common user vehicles with lower fuel mileage values. For vehicles to be used for non-operational duties, electromotive vehicles may be considered. Technological advances have ensured that the latest generation vehicles are more efficient per brake horse power (bhp). Similarly, development of customised electromotive vehicles can be taken up for specific duties of the military. The scope of such vehicles in the Services is quite large but introducing these without a matching maintenance/operations culture would be counter-productive.
- Diesel Generating (DG) sets for power supply to movable communication and radar units. A radical idea, though not in the efficiency realm, would see a renewable energy source like solar being used for supplies to support services of such units like air conditioning and sundry equipment. DG sets for standby power supply to any operational utility or domestic buildings should be selected with energy efficiency norms

as a top consideration. This aspect acquires particular urgency for the sets installed/placed in inhospitable terrain or far-flung locations that require special maintenance support, whether all year long or during specific months. The cost of supplying fuel in these places makes it mandatory that efficiency norms i.e to ensure better fuel efficiency for these DG sets are actively enforced.

- Refrigerators and deep freezers that are purchased in a decentralised manner for messes and gyms, including the exercise equipment, equipment that is installed in many defence welfare ventures. All such equipment comprises mostly off-the-shelf purchases and, thus, just purchasing a higher energy rating product would meet the need of achieving energy efficiency. This point is emphasised because in India, the best and worst possible energy efficiency cases exist together, and this is a strange phenomenon, in that even the worst seems to have a market. In fact, a great opportunity exists presently in the case of this equipment. Most of the refrigerators/chiller plants that were working on CFCs/HCFCs, etc would need to be either retrofitted or replaced as these chemicals are already phased-out or are in the process of being phased-out under the Montreal Protocol on ODS control. Using this opportunity to go for higher energy-efficient equipment as replacements would be a leadership decision that needs to be adopted.
- It has already been recommended in previous chapters that during the procurement of military hardware, Life Cycle Costs (LCC) should be taken into consideration at the comparative process phase of selection. LCC is normally the total cost of owning, operating, and maintaining a system over its total (including extended) life. This approach has now become the norm and is followed even for big ticket purchases by the Indian Air Force like the Medium Multi-Role Combat Aircraft (MMRCA). Energy costs are obviously a part of LCC, hence, if LCC becomes a criterion for induction of all military hardware, the purpose of building energy efficiency in the military would be automatically served. There are a few methods available to compare the energy costs in LCC, for the present as well as in the

future; they take into account the factors used for computing energy costs viz. energy price indices and discount factors to calculate future costs of energy.

- The maintenance procedures for equipment being used in the military need to be so specified that energy efficiency is inbuilt. The testers and powered tools being used for maintenance activities should also be selected based on energy efficiency norms. This is again to be taken into account for the purposes of LCC.
- Even for operational commitments, energy efficiency should be the norm. Consider an aircraft starting aggregates in an air force. These aggregates could be fuel driven or even battery operated as they have to manoeuvre on the tarmac only. The choice of vehicle would depend primarily on operational considerations that should consider the ease of availability of the energy source at different locations as well as the energy efficiency of the two alternatives. In the case of diesel ground power units, the rationale of efficiency of DG sets, as explained above, would apply.

Buildings or Energy Sinks?

The areas covered above are common to all organisations in general and not just the military in specific. The uniqueness is observed in the way the military can achieve these targets by its disciplined way of working. This is evident from the example given below of how the Indian Army has opted for constructing an eco-friendly engineering college building in Pune, India.

Box 1

A Case Study of Energy-Efficient Buildings[10]

The Commandant of the College of Military Engineering (CME), Lt Gen U.S.P. Sinha, on Thursday, inaugurated the green building at the college, which will not only conserve energy but is also fitted with an efficient rainwater harvesting system.

The project has been conceptualised and **planned by the student officers** undergoing degree engineering course at the CME as an "eco-friendly building". The building incorporates various **passive, hybrid and active design strategies to reduce the carbon footprint** of the built form and ensures minimum impact on the environment and contributes positively towards energy efficiency and water conservation. "**Energy efficiency in the building has been achieved through appropriate orientation of the built form to optimise the benefit of reduced solar heat gain and maximise the natural ventilation. The use of natural lighting has been maximised by providing light-shelves. Natural ventilation has been enhanced by use of turbo ventilators and wind towers, in conjunction with the appropriately placed windows. There has been increased use of energy efficient appliances like CFLs/LED lights for lighting and solar heating technology in this building,**" said, a defence spokesperson. "The aspect of water conservation has been taken care of by effective **rainwater harvesting and using water conserving appliances like low flow faucets, dual flush tanks, waterless urinals.** Various **green building materials** incorporated in the construction of this building are **fly-ash bricks, low VOC paints, MDF boards for flooring, doors and furniture,**" he added. The project is an initiative of the college to promote environmental friendly technologies to harness the maximum advantages of nature without causing much disturbance to the ecological balance.

Stating this example here serves a twin purpose. It appropriately summarises the various environmentally friendly and energy efficient practices that can be put in place in a well designed building (mentioned in bold). But the fact that the military has done it without any duress, just to showcase its design abilities and well meaning social responsibility, is a clear pointer that it is ready to follow it through in all aspects of its working; proper motivation and orientation from the top echelon is obviously mandatory.

There are many building standards, national and international, that lay down energy and good design rating for a building.[11] 'Green buildings' by itself is a complete subject that requires very wide coverage, which is not intended here. Suffice to state here that this offers a tremendous opportunity to introduce energy efficiency and conservation measures. In India, green buildings are not yet mandatory but the government departments have to take the lead to ensure that others also follow suit. There are a few facets of energy efficiency and conservation in a building's design that are required to be noted here so that the point is well driven home. These are mentioned below briefly:

- Design for natural lighting during the day; energy efficient lighting in the night.
- Design for ventilation and reduced requirement for air-conditioning; use energy efficient and ODS free air-conditioners when necessary;
- Installation of power management devices; premium efficiency motors, occupancy sensors, high performance windows, daylight dimming, and switching of all loads, however small during non-use.
- There are many construction details like insulation, etc that help in reducing energy usage. These need to be incorporated.

Ease of Solution and Implementation Imperatives

What has been described until now requires only a willing leadership to introduce the efficiency measures in the military. The implementation of energy efficiency projects may be thought of as an abstract action till a well-defined strategy is put in place. The way forward can be accomplished very well with a fine chartered path laid down by the Indian government. The Energy Service Companies (ESCOs) and local governments have partnered to increase energy efficiency. These methodologies are similar to what their counterparts in the US are using and work on the principle of performance contracting instead of adopting the traditional payment route that requires up-front payments, knowing fully well that energy efficiency measures are initially capital-intensive.[12] In the US, ESCOs mainly work under the US Federal Government sponsored Federal Energy Management Programme (FEMP). There are over 100 active ESCOs in the US alone. An

ESCO provides performance and savings guarantees and its remuneration is directly tied to the energy savings achieved either through shared savings or guaranteed savings. There are a few instances of saving in India while working with ESCOs that are given below[13]. This would give any organisation an idea of how to cut costs even while implementing energy efficiency measures.

- In 2001, DSCLES, one of the first ESCOs in India, worked with the New Delhi Municipal Council on a high-efficiency electrical lighting pilot project that now saves 252,000 kWh per year. The project produces savings of US$ 50,000 and CO2 emissions of 149 million tonnes per year were avoided. DSCLES financed the initial investment of US$ 75,000, which means the project's payback period was approximately 18 months. This makes marked business sense for both entities.
- **Asian Electronics** replaced approximately 12,000 tube lights at the Sachivalaya Complex for the government of **Gujarat, at Gandhinagar**, with energy-efficient alternatives which reduced the lighting load by 64 percent without sacrificing illumination levels.
- In the state of **Tamil Nadu** in India, a municipal energy efficiency programme partnering with ESCOs was underway in 29 cities.

If the situation made complete business sense, which it does, then this partnership should have seen very wide implementation. Some reasons for not observing a wide movement on this front could be: (a) an inertia on the part of users/facility to feel the urgent need for energy efficiency as it may be of low priority compared to other critical and pressing objectives; (b) actual lack of technical information on the potential saving and image enhancement that can accrue due to this partnership or the choices available; (c) resistance to change is a mindset issue that needs to be tackled as owners would have to cast themselves in a long-term partnership with the ESCO; (d) the highest management is not interested in the objective of energy efficiency due to lack of interest or dearth of information; (e) specific to the military, any ESCO cannot be invited to enter the military installations as it has security implications that need to be suitably addressed, thus, requiring a government's administrative intervention. It should also be understood that it is not always that an ESCO would finance the projects and that various other options are available in the market.

Energy Efficiency: A Panacea for All?

After understanding the business case of energy efficiency, it is natural to question whether energy efficiency can lead to energy saving? If this is the case, then most of the issues involved in reducing energy consumption would be suitably addressed, finally allowing the technology to sever the cord connecting quality of life and energy; a connection very well debated in George Monbiot's path breaking book *Heat: How To Stop The Planet From Burning*[14] and then recommending some technical fixes on carbon sequestration. However, even he has admitted that the only way to save carbon emissions in aviation is to fly less (Chapter 9) or in the context of this chapter, conserve energy. As John Foster has said, *"Downshifting à la carte from the option-menu available, even if it is done society-wide, may alleviate immediately uncomfortable symptoms to the point at which they are bearable, but leave the disease itself essentially unremedied."*[15] Reducing consumption is, therefore, an imperative for resource optimisation.

There is another important factor to be kept in mind while implementing energy efficiency policies called the rebound effect associated with such measures. What it implies is essentially that as the technological and other measures to enhance energy efficiency are undertaken, the benefits are offset by behavioural changes in the users that negate the energy or resources saved due to higher efficiency. Roughly, the rebound effect means that if the energy bill is going to be the same, the user is likely to feel, "Why not use more appliances or drive more for more material benefits?"[16] The jury is still out with regards to the rebound effect and we can relate to it by our own experiences. It is but certain that for the military to reduce its dependence on energy, only energy efficiency would not be able to fit the bill. Considering the arguments described here, it is now clear that militaries would have to act on energy conservation simultaneously (along with energy efficiency) if the real benefits of resource optimisation are to be derived. Conservation is more complex than mere technical fixes leading to efficiency. It calls for deep-rooted changes and cultural shifts. In the context of the military, both of these are very difficult and so making a business case of the same is essential. The following section attempts to do the same.

The Last Bastion: Energy Conservation

Energy conservation in the context of this chapter implies actually reducing energy consumption levels. To the extent energy efficiency also leads to reduction in consumption, it is a conservation strategy. However, as already mentioned, I would treat conservation differently from efficiency. Energy conservation/reduction can be brought about by two ways. The first one is through equipment change – to that which will consume less or be more energy-efficient. This aspect has already been covered earlier in the chapter. The second path emphasises actually modifying technology and working processes to achieve reduction in energy usage. Within the military, technological improvements are an ongoing process for obvious operational reasons and, thus, this offers low-hanging fruit for including the energy conservation mindset as a part of such improvements.

Modification of processes is a different challenge altogether. The set pattern of military working is difficult to change. The rationale for such changes has to be very coherent and not merely personality driven because in the event of the latter, there is always a chance that such processes will revert to the original ways once the driver of the change is no longer present. So any modification suggested has to make eminent business sense. While this is logical, it removes out-of-the-box process modifications straight away from the table. Normally, such thinking does not strike an immediate chord due to the uniqueness of the ideas and within the military it will still take longer to convince the leadership about the efficacy of the suggestions. So most of the cases mentioned here are those that have been implemented successfully in one organisation or the other.

The first stage of conservation really starts with managing your existing inventory well. A view of the power inventory in a military installation can be taken by application of meters and/or sub-meters to identify the energy cost saving accruing out of conservation ventures. This would also allow a system of energy audits to be put in place; without audits, the efficacy of the entire programme cannot be known, corrective actions cannot be instituted and the weak links would never get exposed. Only if the metering is not cost-effective can an engineering extrapolation be carried out for an installation considering the loads installed therein. Certain features in the military's operational scenarios that save power/fuel (two main sources of energy consumption) with the use of technological 'fixes' are briefly outlined below. Conservation of energy in buildings has already been covered earlier.

- Use of right size chillers/heating devices. This has been noticed as one of the common causes of extra energy consumption. It is easy to install the right size provided the quantitative requirements are clearly spelt out at the time of provisioning.
- Use of compressors (for filling air in cylinders, etc.) strictly on requirement basis. Air filling in cylinders is normally outsourced but when it is done in-house, its operation should be carefully monitored.
- Use of Light Emitting Diodes (LEDs), a semi-conductor based lighting in place of normal lighting of offices, large warehouses and operations hub centres has many advantages over conventional lighting sources. With the advent of organic LEDs, it is becoming increasing environmentally friendly and with increase in their numbers, the costs are also on their way down. Higher life and almost no maintenance also go in favour of changing over to this light source that consumes almost 70 percent less energy as compared to a normal light source[17] with the life cycle costs in its favour. LED lighting would also be utilised increasingly in illumination of cockpit avionics for obvious advantages of lesser energy loads on limited power supply available in the aircraft.
- Air operations use the largest amount of fuel despite the advent of higher by-pass aero-engines that provide for more thrust per litre of fuel used and are, thus, more economical. Optimisation of fuel use in aviation would remain a high priority area for conserving energy. This optimisation can be brought about by stringent mission planning and execution[18]. Procurement of aircraft that use less fuel by the use of the latest technology of design and composites, etc. is a technological fix of green procurements. But if one was to consider George Monbiot's[19] analyses, it would be clear that aviation *per se* would not permit an enhanced reduction in fuel consumption. The alternative suggested is to

fly less – possible only to a certain extent for the military if it converts some amount of its training on to simulators; or use ground transport for short haul movements.

- Use of early and advanced warning systems, and precision-guided munitions and advanced avionics have improved the mission capabilities, thus, allowing for more missions to deliver as planned. Optimising routing and flying profiles would also lead to reduction of fuel wastages. There is always a potential to save fuel by improving mission planning. On more than one occasion, mission completion at any cost – in short, mission-fixation – narrows the view so as to remove the focus from the larger picture. It is here that capacity-building and enhancing awareness can play a major role. The military leaders may also be provided with technology like mission planning computers that would assist them in optimising the flight and route planning. Use of such technological inputs provides an opportunity for simplifying the planning process and making it less time-consuming.
- Simulators have a big role to play in conserving resources. Innovative use of flight simulators results in more than just fuel conservation. For example, flight simulators assist in conserving airframe life due to fewer hours flown for training; and, reduce the number of aircraft utilised for training, which frees them for actual operational missions. Simulators also help in fine-tuning the raw edges in a trainee as an analysis of his/her actions is easy, with all actions being supervised and recorded. Even the training standards may rise in a few instances with the use of simulators – a win-win situation. So use of simulators should be set as a priority through laid-down targets. The targets can be laid down as per the organisational requirement; the quantum is not so important as sticking to these targets is essential.
- Air refuelling has become a force multiplier in today's battle space. These missions are regularly practised wherein the aircraft refueller and the receiver aircraft take off from different airfields. It is important to coordinate the status of such sorties to ensure that missions are not cancelled due to unserviceability at any end. A point to be noted here is that air refuelling is a costly (with fully burdened cost of fuel criteria) and fuel-intensive affair;

so it would be prudent to have en route fuel stops as the norm, unless the mission specifically requires the format of refuelling.

- There is not only the potential of saving aviation fuel but vehicle fuel (especially in the Army) can also be conserved with a careful planning and auditing exercise. Induction of fuel-efficient vehicles has already been covered earlier. But what also needs to be kept in mind is that the vehicles that come back after major repairs should not have become inefficient. This would imply that a performance check needs to be done for fuel efficiency and if the cost-benefit figures are in favour, the inefficient vehicle may be taken off road.

From the above, it must be clear that technology is as important as proper planning for equipment utilisation to optimise energy usage. Planning and then auditing the implementation of actions taken actually amount to the process of energy management. This is a desired feature for any organisation that wants to maximise its gains. In the course of equipment evaluation for energy consumption, there may be cases wherein the capital costs of procurement of energy efficient equipment may be high. At this point, it needs to be asked: are these costs justified (not only from the point of view of life cycle) for ensuring that resources so saved are available for actual needs, if and when they so arise? In the case of the military, this need may occur on the breakout of actual hostilities. Availability of scarce resources as well as lower dependence on these are essentially two sides of the same coin that can make all the difference between losing and winning a war.

The starting point for these ventures on energy conservation would remain taking stock of the total energy consumption – power and fuel – within the military. Without clear-cut statistics of the energy being consumed in different areas of military operations, the strategies that would be framed for conservation and/or moving to renewable sources, would not be effective. These figures are also required for planning a sustained operation/mission/campaign and, thus, should be regarded as a significant planning tool for the military's operations. The statistics on energy consumption (both fuel and electricity) would not be generated without a direction from the top management. As already mentioned earlier, the MoD is not a line ministry for the MoEF or the Planning Commission for assessing/communicating their own energy needs and then working towards reducing their green house gas emissions. So the chief driver for the development of figures of consumption would have to be emerge from inside the organisation only. A comparison of energy consumption of the Army, the Air Force and the Navy should be carried out while compiling the pan-MoD figures. Within the individual Services, these figures of consumption should be for operational use of military hardware (ground/air/sea); utilities – operational and domestic; and for ground support equipment/operations (as an example, for the Air Force, vehicle fuel consumption would come under the head of support equipment). There are no stringent boundaries for compilation of these figures. It is essential to include all sources of energy consumption to arrive at a holistic picture and for taking conservation and conversion (to renewable sources) decisions. A true leadership action would be to break down the operational energy consumption figures to understand the consumption trends minutely, a study that would come in handy for campaign planning too. For example, in the case of an air force, fuel figures for fighters, bombers, trainers, air maintenance and support aviation activities (including communication) should be compiled separately with respect to total sorties and number of hours of flying generated. This would give us a synopsis of energy use of the air force and the avenues of energy reduction attempts.

Renewable Sources of Energy in the Military

It would also be worthwhile to mention the use of renewable sources of energy, which should be considered at par with conservation of energy, not just because renewable sources of energy are environmentally friendly but also due to the fact that they offer an additional source of off-grid energy, which is important for remote and rugged terrains. Use of renewable sources in a few cases may also be economical. Consider the use of solar lights for lighting the runway in an airfield that does not require underground cabling (and its maintenance). This is being done at major airfields[20] like Elmendorf Air Force Base in Alaska, in the US, where the extreme environment, electricity costs, breakdowns and remote locations offer an ideal opportunity for using "off the shelf" solar LED airfield lights. There are air force bases of the United States Air Force (USAF) that have their own solar power generation systems. In December 2007, the US Air Force commissioned the largest photovoltaic solar array in the Americas (14.2 megawatts) at Nellis Air Force Base. This supports about one-fourth of the base's energy usage per day and has an estimated annual cost savings of $1 million. Also, in the year 2007, the USAF continued to lead the US federal government in green power purchases, with 37 bases meeting some portion of their base-wide electrical requirements from commercial sources of wind, solar, geothermal or biomass.[21] This opportunity exists at many remote military bases in India because of abundance of sunlight, harsh environment and almost non-existent power grid.

Use of solar or wind power for remote locations is eminently achievable. A slightly out of the box action would be to come up with energy sources for the military that makes it optimally utilise all resources at its command for generating power. Consider the example given below, in Box 2. This example will prove that solutions for the use of all resources at the command of the military, actually have greater benefits in operational scenarios. Since the militaries exist for undertaking operations, they need to really come up with such solutions that allow them flexibility without sacrificing commitment.

Box 2[22]

An Example of Innovative Energy Generation In Field Conditions

The US Army's Rapid Equipping Force had deployed two Tactical Garbage to Energy Refineries (TGER) in Iraq for a capability demonstration. TGER converts field waste (paper, plastic, cardboard and food slop) into biofuel that is used to power a 60 kilowatt generator. A battalion sized forward operating base (600-800 soldiers) creates about one ton of garbage per day that can be recycled into energy, so the system is designed to convert 1 ton of waste into energy...

In aviation (both civil and military), the Western governments are actively propagating use of alternate fuels. The USAF has even set a target for increasing the use of alternate fuel for their operations every year. In the same context, the possibility of using alternatively-powered ground equipment and vehicles needs to be explored. An example of the same has been given earlier for aircraft starting trolleys. This can be extended for vehicles that would not be deployed for operational commitments. A case in point is the buses being run by Karnataka State Road Transport Corporation (KSRTC). These have converted to a diesel blend for all the buses in their inventory. Reduction of costs and protection of the environment have been the natural byproducts. Spread over a large geographical location, the supply of diesel blend to all the depots of the state was a challenge that was overcome with planning and passion. KSRTC, being a state government department, could still do it on account of innovative thinking and the commitment shown by its top management. This can be transposed within the non-operational framework of the military too.

Converting to renewable sources for the military has to be a planned effort. It will need to be studied whether the conversion process degrades or adds to the operational effectiveness; whether there is a chance of exploitation of this usage by the adversary; and the comparative costs and ease of operation. For example the rotating magnets in the turbine electrical generator (of a wind turbine) produce a low level of electromagnetic interference that can affect television and radio signals within two-three km of large installations. This does not affect line-of-sight microwave satellite transmission.[23] It is beyond the purview of this chapter to provide these cost-comparative figures as most of these are customised solutions specific to the location and type of renewable source envisaged. It would be worthwhile to state that in almost all these cases, the initial costs of installation would be higher than conventional sources.

Research and Development

The Defence Research and Development Organisation (DRDO) labs work on defence technology. It is an MoD sub-department in India. They are the appropriate agencies that can be tasked for suggesting innovative processes for energy conservation in equipment. They can also work on providing renewable energy solutions specific to military operations.

Since their personnel are security cleared, it would be easier for them to perform trials of technology/equipment being developed by them at remote, deployed locations of the military installations. DRDO would also be in a good position to partner with private companies to integrate cutting-edge technologies in the field operations of the military.

It is difficult to suggest areas in the military where renewable energy sources can be utilised. The scope is wide as the military is an energy intensive organisation and, in India, solar energy and biomass are abundantly available. With the principle of demand and supply totally in favour of such forays by DRDO, some of the fields that they can focus on are the customisation of solar PV panels for rugged field conditions; mobile solar energy generators for Rajasthan and Ladakh area; biomass energy converters for central and eastern India; mobile cooled accommodation for troops and solar panels for running air-conditioners in utilities located in airfields in remote locations. Another area of focussed research can be more efficient, long-lasting and lighter battery systems that can significantly improve the mission effectiveness and mobility of a soldier. Research into advanced battery technologies can be pursued actively by DRDO with the probable involvement of the Ministry of New and Renewable Energy (MNRE).

A take-off from the field of advanced battery technology can be the requirement to pair rechargeable batteries with renewable energy technologies to extend a soldier's range and effectiveness. In this area, fuel cells technology will become ubiquitous in the times to come as a source of portable power for troops. Fuel cells use gas as a means of generating electrical energy rather than a liquid or solid. It is much more efficient than even an internal combustion engine. Its electricity production effectiveness is said to be more than 60 percent and it does not produce any noise. Fuel cells are costly and would need a hydrogen distribution network for their sustenance. But if their usage can be extended to vehicles and similar wide use applications, their management would become easy and, thus, this needs to be seriously considered in the gamut of the renewable energy revolution. These are only a few places where renewable sources can be developed for the military. There are many readymade solutions that may be used albeit with minor variations. The challenge would remain to develop pan-military solutions.

Innovations for reducing energy consumption would be considered force multipliers as they would allow increasing the flexibility of undertaking missions by the military. The R&D authorities, thus, need to consider this actively in their calculus of priorities, which at present do not find a bold mention in their list of activities displayed on their website.[24] For the sake of analysis only, one may compare the Defence Advanced Research Projects Agency (DARPA) of the US that has many energy efficiency and conservation projects running as well as successfully concluded. These projects range from investigating the suitability of new bio fuels, innovative technologies for assured Arctic awareness, to finding high efficiency solar cells.[25] The brand value and scope of DRDO need to be suitably altered by venturing into such advanced and challenging fields.

The Long and Short of it……

The military, like any other large organisation, would need energy to perform its mandated tasks. There is no getting around it! However, what any organisation can do is to reduce its energy bills by resorting to some technical innovations in equipment use and process modifications. It is more a matter of change in the mindset that is required rather than only hunting for solutions as the technology is changing at a fast pace, with energy efficiency and conservation becoming the trend. The costs and benefits of such changes do matter but for the military they have a far more profound effect. With reduction in energy requirement for undertaking the same quantum of missions, the military is not only helping the environment but also helping itself become more potent. Since a majority of energy sources are fossil fuel-based, exposing the military to the vagaries of changes being seen in the international oil market is like playing with national security. So a business case exists for reducing the fossil fuel dependence of the military.

Energy dependence is reduced by resorting to efficiency and conservation measures simultaneously. This is true for any organisation. For the military, it may be comparatively easier to in-build energy efficiency by introducing such equipment. However, even for this, the traditional mindset has to be changed and procurement procedures modified. For conservation or reducing energy consumption, it would be necessary to modify existing processes and upgrade to a higher level of technology. This is where the role of R&D agencies becomes important. It is my firm belief that technological innovations are the foundation of nation-building. Interpolating it for the Indian military, it can easily be seen that the DRDO has a major role to play. Since the DRDO is meant to equip the military with the latest technologies and equipment, it is essential that they venture into energy efficiency technologies through whatever means are open to them. The cascading effects that such endeavours would have on the civil sector can only prove beneficial in the national development process.

Renewable sources of energy are being actively pursued in India with a separate ministry looking after their usage (MNRE). It is surprising to see that one of the largest ministries (MoD) is not really on board in implementing these vital technologies of the future. Renewable sources of energy like solar or bio-mass have a huge potential in India. If the military opts for off-grid generation of renewable energy for its far-flung and deployed locations it would give it an additional option without bothering about disruption of grid supplies. The flexibility of planning operations with your own energy supply is a huge bonus.

Fuel supplies for ground transportation are also a precious resource that need to be guarded well during hostilities. The reserves that have to be deployed for this can be gainfully used for other activities. Lower dependence on fuel can only be brought about with the use of highly efficient vehicles, careful planning and use of alternative energy sources for vehicles. These are mostly achievable technological solutions provided the higher echelons of the military leadership take it up as a challenge today. Tomorrow may be too late and there is always a chance that post-2020, when India would have to undertake verifiable carbon emission cuts, the Services would also be called to play their part. Then they might have to approach the government for exemptions, citing various contingencies, the way it is being done in the US, without much success. It is better to wake up to that reality now and work towards it so that the leadership that the military displays on this front can set an example for other government departments too.

Notes

1. http://data.undp.org.in/ene_pub/NATCOM.pdf, accessed on February 9, 2012. This informs of India's Second National Communication to the UNFCCC – Work Programme.
2. http://europa.eu/legislation_summaries/energy/energy_efficiency/l27057_en.htm accessed on January 18, 2012. For the US DoD national legislation exemptions, refer "Exemptions from Environmental Law for the Department of Defense: An Overview of Congressional Action." See http://www.sixwise.com/pdf/RS22149.pdf, accessed on February 20, 2012.
3. ODS are substances that deplete the stratospheric ozone layer, which safeguards the earth from harmful ultra violet radiations.
4. http://e360.yale.edu/feature/new_mission_for_us_military_breaking_its_dependence_on_oil/2348/, accessed on January 18, 2012.
5. The US federal funds are allotted for energy conservation in the overall scheme. See http://www.geconsumerandindustrial.com/environmentalinfo/regulations_resources/pop_efficiency_provisions_federal_buildings.htm, accessed on January 18, 2012.
6. Energy intensity is defined as energy use per unit of GDP by the UN. Quantum of GDP is a measure of national economic strength. See http://www.un.org/esa/sustdev/natlinfo/indicators/isdms2001/isd-ms2001economicB.htm, accessed on February 22, 2012. In the Indian context, the Planning Commission's report on low carbon growth can be seen at http://planningcommission.nic.in/reports/genrep/Inter_Exp.pdf, accessed on February 16, 2012.
7. H.D. Kumar, *Energy and Natural Resources: Sustainability and Management* (New Delhi: Vitasta Publishing Pvt Ltd, 2008), p. 32.
8. "Chinese Military Improves Energy Efficiency to Help Achieve National Emissions Target," an article dated February 10, 2012. See http://www.theclimategroup.org/our-news/news/2012/2/10/chinese-military-improves-energy-efficiency-to-help-achieve-national-emissions-targets/, accessed on February 24, 2012.
9. n. 6.
10. "Military Engineering College gets an Eco-Friendly Building," Express News Service (Pune), April 16, 2010. See http://www.indianexpress.com/news/military-engg-college-gets-an-ecofriendly-b/607031/, accessed on February 25, 2012
11. Some of the sites that can be visited for additional reading on green buildings in defence are listed here. See http://www.hrgbc.org/presentations/gim_presentations/Rudy%20Perkey%20-%20Greening%20the%20Military%20II%20%20%28Draft%202009-01-27%29.pdf, accessed on February 1, 2012. http://www.eere.energy.gov/topics/buildings.html, accessed on February 1, 2012.
12. "Energy Efficiency in India: Part 2" by Chandan Singh, on April 10, 2009. See World

Resource Institute site http://www.wri.org/stories/2009/04/energy-efficiency-india-part-2, accessed on February 23, 2012.

13. Ibid.
14. George Monboit, *Heat: How to Stop The Planet From Burning: Love Miles* (Canada: Doubleday, 2006), Chapter 9.
15. John Foster, *The Sustainability Mirage: Illusion and Reality in the Coming War on Climate Change* (London: Earthscan, 2008), pp. 85-86.
16. Monboit, n.14, pp. 61-2. Monbiot has also described Khazzoom-Brookes postulates that describe the idea that energy efficiency gains, paradoxically, result in increases in energy use.
17. Interaction with Dr H.K. Dwivedi, Head R&D, Samtel Corporation on March 27, 2012 at a seminar on MRO in New Delhi.
18. For more on integrated mission planning, readers may visit http://www.mputtre.com/id8.html, accessed on March 29, 2012.
19. Monboit, n.14, Chapter 9.
20. For more information, readers may visit http://www.carmanah.com/aviation-and-obstruction-lighting, accessed on February 8, 2012.
21. http://www.dod.mil/ddre/doc/DoD_Energy_Security_Task_Force.pdf, accessed on October 05, 2012. For use of renewable energy sources in the year 2009 in the US military, readers may wish to refer http://www.acq.osd.mil/ie/energy/library/aemr_fy_09_may_2010.pdf, accessed on March 29, 2012.
22. Ibid.
23. David Pimentel, Marcia H. Pimentel, *Food, Energy, and Society*, Third Edition (US, Boca Raton: CRC Press, 2008), p. 264.
24. http://drdo.gov.in/drdo/English/index.jsp?pg=homebody.jsp, accessed on March 31, 2012.
25. For more information on the work being undertaken by DARPA, readers may visit their website http://www.darpa.mil/Our_Work/STO/Focus_Areas/Energy_and_SelfSufficient_Operations.aspx, accessed on April 2, 2012.

8

Efficiency Through Environmental Audit

Environment Management System

The management process has three broad phases – planning, execution and controlling. There are a few more stages in the process but the three phases mentioned above are distinct and major milestones desired during the setting up of a system; these are also essential for running it efficiently and effectively. In this context, environmental forays also require a systemic management approach in any organisation. The aspects of planning and execution, including the areas where environment management needs to be built in the ethos of the military, have already been covered in the earlier chapters. This, being a new frontier of challenge for the military, would require constant fine-tuning. Therefore, it is essential to craft a feedback loop from the execution phase to the planning phase – this feedback is provided by performing an audit during the execution phase. This is a common practice for enhancing the efficiency of all systems, including military operations and, therefore, is not restricted to environment policies alone. Within the military, this is conventionally performed for day-to-day activities as also to check the operational preparedness of the formations.

In the context of the military, an environmental audit would assess the nature and extent of harm to the environment caused by a particular action or group of activities. This would also check if the desired organisational orientation towards resource efficiency has been achieved by the formation being audited, in line with the organisational orders. The by-product of resource efficiency and also waste management in the formation would automatically result in protection of the environment. The auditor would, thus, also have to observe that such actions are being implemented in the manner and spirit by which they are part of the larger picture of protecting the environment. Using the audit as a feedback tool would help in the following:

- Assessment of how the formation is managing or influencing the condition of the environment, local or otherwise.
- Prioritisation of actions carried out to reduce the impact on the environment.
- Generation of confidence amongst the leadership about the efficacy of policies implemented for resource efficiency.
- Finally, demonstration of accountability to third parties such as government, industry and the denizens of the country that the military leadership is alive to the global challenge of managing the environment.

This chapter would not only try to cover the essence of an environmental audit of a formation but also suggest ways as to how this can be performed in the constricted realm of the military environment. The focus would be on the activities to be audited in a formation, orientation of the agency performing the audit as also the training of auditors and follow-up of the audit process. Though the process would be focussed on a military formation, it would be clear to the discerning eye that extending the process to an industrial environment would not be difficult owing to the many similarities between the two. The scope of the audit would not cover every policy that is issued by the military, in the framework of its environmental impacts. Such an act would be counter-productive and seriously inhibit the military from its operational role. Therefore, the areas specified in this chapter alone should be open for an environmental audit with one odd exception, which may be decided by the highest echelons of the military organisation.

Need for Environmental Audit in Military

The need for environmental audits in any organisation is directly related to the benefits that accrue from such an activity. More than the benefits, there may actually be a legal requirement that necessitates an environmental audit. Both these aspects need to be analysed when deciding upon the priority that environmental audits deserve in an organisation.

The military has been for far too long, cocooned in its specific role of guarding national boundaries. The government on its part has never included the military under the ambit of environmental acts. It is also very clear that at no stage is it specified out of it as well. For example, cutting down of trees of more than a certain girth inside an Air Force formation, even for operational reasons, requires specific permissions from the forest department officials and these laws are equally applicable to all. The fact that the military has not been audited by the governmental agencies on environmental matters, may have led to non-realisation of the impact of these legislations on their operations. This statement bears scrutiny when we consider the stipulations of the Montreal Protocol that specifically required the member parties to adhere to the 'no production and consumption of ODS' regime. National legislation in India also supported this as the country is a signatory to the Protocol. Uninformed of these stipulations as well as of the harm that the actions of emitting the ODS into the atmosphere cause, the Indian military was doing so while maintaining its ODS-based hardware. It continued to rely on ODS supplies, little realising that these would not be available any more due to the production ban (from January 1, 2010) on them throughout the world. Even the procurement of military hardware till recently, did not carry a condition of non-ODS dependency. Finally, the leadership did realise the need for their phase-out and as an interim measure till alternatives are in place, is conserving these vital chemicals and resorting to recycling and reuse.

Another benefit that accrues due to an environmental audit is to highlight areas of inefficiency in processes, for example, where the resources used are disproportional to the output produced. By identifying operational inefficiencies, the organisation may be able to reduce costs and/or improve its environmental performance. Military hardware and vehicle maintenance activities utilising consumable spares, mineral oils and lubes, if not audited and if the consumption level is not monitored through scientific means, can turn out to be a costly affair that is capable of harming the environment as well. The performance standards can easily be benchmarked by considering the use of resources for the same or similar output or even while comparing the implementation of the two processes. Consider the example given in the box below that easily brings out the effect the environment audit process can bring out. This example is based on a 'one off' environment audit that was carried out by the author.

Box 1

When a component fails, prematurely, while fitted on/to a military hardware, it is returned to the overhaul agency for investigation. The rationale is to learn from the failure and recommend or implement remedial measures to avoid premature failures. It is obvious that premature failures cost money as well as affect the operational efficiency due to the downtime of hardware. These components are returned on a prescribed form describing the condition of the failure and some more details that would allow the repair agency to correctly assess the cause of failure.

During an audit comparison of two formations using the same type and quantity of military hardware, in a similar geographical environment, it was realised that the number of failures reported by one formation was 12 times more than the other on a monthly basis. This pointed to either one of the formations not filling up the required form or actually its failure rate being that much lower. Both of these required further checks and, hence, necessary remedial action was initiated. What emerges from this case is that a normal process audit resulting in resource efficiency can as well be a part of an environmental audit as, finally, the common minimum objective in both remains higher efficiency; the higher objective in the latter also being protection of the environment.

In the same vein as above, use of consumable spares and materials for a system that is being introduced newly in the organisation needs to be done judiciously. The initial benchmarking, if not done properly, may result in over or underprovisioning, both of which have critical repercussions for a military organisation and the environment – specifically in the case of overprovisioning. A product based process audit is customarily a norm for such introductions and it revolves around operational and technology absorption. An environmental audit can also be dovetailed in it to learn from the Original Equipment Manufacturer (OEM) how to optimise the system with the least inputs, and life cycle savings ensured. This should be consciously introduced as a part of all new systems.

Another need of an environmental audit is reduction in risk that accrues from environmental degradation. The risk involved when the formation is dealing with hazardous polluting substances, like in the case of a military formation, can expose it to a public backlash as well as cause legal complications. Compliance status and judging public perception are all part of an environmental audit. There have been instances wherein the local community has vented its exasperation when it has been confronted by military training activities. This has been noticed near armament ranges, specifically when the community has been allowed to settle down closer than permissible limits to these installations, due to various social causative factors. The actions taken by the local formation to firstly not allow this situation to take place and, secondly, to retrieve the situation if the settlement has already taken place, need to be constantly audited for intervention, at the appropriate level and time.

Dimensions of Environmental Audit

At present, two types of environmental audits are prevalent internationally. The first one is known as 'compliance audit' and the second is called 'system audit'. The first type of audit, as the name suggests, is carried out to confirm that the organisation being audited is compliant of existing rules/policies/ instructions/legislations on the environment. One example of this has already been given in the second chapter where it has been shown how the waste disposal in military formations has to be compliant with the legislation on the subject. There are other areas too where organisational instructions exist, for example, the management of Ozone Depleting Substances (ODS) or disposal of e-waste, etc, that need to be complied with. A detailed activity list for carrying out a compliance audit would be mentioned later in the chapter. The compliance status needs to be checked periodically not only to see the effort put in by the formation but, more importantly, to see the practicality of the implementation procedures devised thereafter. Thus, it is an important feedback loop for fine-tuning the formulation of policies, or in other words, the planning process.

The other type of audit that is performed is the 'management system' audit. Again, as the name suggests, this type of audit is performed to facilitate management control of day-to-day practices which may have an impact on the environment. This would also include the impact of operational activities on the community within the geographical proximity to the formation. This is a very important aspect of socially demonstrable behaviour showcasing the leadership that the military can display in managing the environment. Its operational connotations are obvious as the military formations are always supported by the local communities for a variety of activities, through thick and thin.

There is one more type of audit that may be warranted at least in the initial stages of setting up the environmental management system within the military or in any other organisation. Since this is not a part of the regular environment audit process, it should be treated separately and only performed at a distinct stage of policy-making. This audit activity mainly pertains to assessing and reviewing the activities of the policy-makers like setting up objectives, services, and laying down policies and instructions. Since these activities would be predominantly performed by the highest echelons when the system is being set up, this audit function would provide them inputs on a likely policy impact assessment. The methodology to perform the initial environment policy impact assessment audit is very different from the compliance and management system audits. The policy impact assessment can also be extended to include the site or equipment audit, wherein an audit of a particular site/equipment to examine actual or potential environmental problems in selecting that particular site or equipment, is carried out. The difference in these audits emanates primarily from the level of an audit, its objectives as well as the results envisaged being of conceptual nature in the case of audit wherein the policy-making itself is audited. The box below is a case study of an equipment audit being carried out in the US Army. This would give the readers an idea on how the compliance, management and policy audits are interlinked at a certain level.

Box 2[1]

The Programmatic Environmental Assessment (PEA) evaluates potential direct, indirect and cumulative effects of Military Police (MP) companies and platoons using the M117 Armoured Security Vehicle (ASV) at Army installations in the United States. A MP Combat Support Company is authorised 47 High Mobility Multi-purpose Wheeled Vehicles (HMMWV); the MP Platoon organic to a Brigade Combat Team is authorised 14 HMMWVs. The Army plans to equip each MP Company with 12 ASVs and each MP Platoon organic to Brigade Combat Teams with six ASVs. For each ASV it receives, a unit will exchange one HMMWV. There will be no net increase of vehicles or of personnel assigned an MP unit receiving the ASV. A total of 3,118 ASVs are scheduled to be distributed to MP units Army-wide.

Because the proposed action will be to use the ASV at Army installations nationwide, the Army is analyzing the action in a programmatic approach. Subsequent site-specific NEPA (National Environmental Policy Act of 1969) analysis may be conducted at installations where MP units are assigned .....To facilitate proper use of this PEA, as well as compliance with the President's Council for Environmental Quality (CEQ) guidance and the Army's regulations governing NEPA, the Army has provided a Record of Environmental Consideration (REC) checklist that provides a framework for identifying NEPA requirements beyond the scope of PEA. If the conditions of this checklist are met, and if procedures and mitigations are adopted at the installation level, an REC may be prepared that references this PEA and the proposed action may proceed.

Environmental audits have mostly dealt with the environmental effects of industrial operations, maintenance and administrative processes. To a lesser extent, they have also dealt with building efficiency in resource consumption. Guided by the legislation and compliance procedures, the environment has traditionally been considered in terms of air, land and water. Building resource efficiency has never claimed dominance while designing such audit programmes as this aspect has all along been considered a by-product of process or regular audits. Auditing is always carried out to check the efficacy of systems that have been put in place, to observe if they are having the desired effect and helping the organisation achieve its objectives. Within the military, these audits usually give scant regard to achieving a cost reduction process that consumes few resources and thereby also protects the environment. While the operational features of a new system being introduced in the military are discussed threadbare, its overall resource saving potential is seldom open for consideration because that does not get prioritised in the organisational objectives. This approach would need to change within the military and is actually changing everywhere due to the prevailing economic conditions (2008 onwards) across the globe.

The audit that the organisation decides to conduct may include elements of all three types of audit mentioned earlier. Environmental audits can be modified according to the size and complexity of the formation being audited. For example, a static unit dealing with only logistics may simply concentrate on waste reuse and disposal, water usage and energy consumption, whereas an operational formation may have a broader range of systems (including the ones just mentioned) to be measured. Common areas for analysis in an environmental audit would include the following:

- Materials usage: parsimony in consumption.
- Energy consumption patterns.
- Water consumption patterns and reuse/recycle methodologies.
- Emissions, industrial effluents and waste management.
- Compliance with environmental rules, policies and instructions.
- Transport usage and optimisation.
- Total environmental protection expenditures and green building forays.
- Impact on local community, including biodiversity.

International Trends in Environment Audits

Environment audits are now a norm in almost all the countries that are trying to make a mark in environmental diplomacy. These are being carried out in the industry as a part of their Corporate Environment Responsibility (CER) as also to avoid any non-compliance, legal complications. The boost in public image and enhanced cost benefits are no doubt a big driving force behind such decisions by the corporate world. However, it is seen that increasingly the militaries in the developed countries are concerned and working on a system of environment management, with environment audit as a major part of it. For example, the US Army has a US Army Environmental Command (USAEC)[2] that takes care of an extensive environmental programme of the US Army ranging from sustainability issues, compliance, forestry, and pollution prevention to technology and human/cultural resources. The US DoD also has its own Environmental Assessment and Management (TEAM) Guide. The US system also has the US Environmental Protection Agency's (US EPA's) generic protocol for conducting environmental audits of federal facilities, besides the International Standardisation Organisation's (ISO's) Standard 14001 being followed in DoD facilities.

The Canadian military has an ongoing programme on environmental audits[3]. The Latvian military's approach to environmental issues also mentions its audit as a major activity to be carried out for the success of the programme[4]. There are many other military organisations that have implemented environmental programmes for reasons of compliance or beyond compliance organisational responsibility. But the distinct commonalities amongst all these programmes are: (a) a policy that is specified on the subject by the top leadership of the organisation; and (b) an audit programme to verify the optimum implementation of the policies. The implementation programmes and focus areas keep varying a little from country to country owing to the peculiarity of locations and operations. It is, thus, an essential requirement to lay down the policy framework on environmental matters in the military. This framework has to be overarching so as to cover all the three pillars of a military organisation – operations, maintenance and administration. It has to be understood that environmental considerations encompass activities being performed in all these spheres and, thus, need audits to see their effective implementation. This is typically the approach that is being followed by the militaries of the developed nations.

Present System of Audit in the IAF

The present system of operational audits in the IAF is a very structured and well tested one that has been periodically modified to be in line with the changes taking place in the organisational outlook. It is a tiered system that focusses on core competency of the formation being audited. The tiered system ensures that the auditing processes of the lower tiers also get audited. The lowest tier consists of the audit team within the formation itself. This team checks all operational and support activities undertaken in the formation on a periodic basis. The scope of the audit is quite broad and it loosely follows the checklist that is used by the audit agency at the top of the pyramid. The focus, as with all the tiers, is on increasing the operational efficiency of the formation. The periodicity of audit is normally quarterly but the process is more or less continuous. Since the audit team is within the formation, the audit is more of an informal interaction that takes place between the operators and their auditing colleagues. The audit report also stays within the formation and the formation commander institutes remedial measures. The issues that get reflected through these audits are more of routine nature and rarely require systemic changes. These reports are also cross-checked by the higher tiers of audit, basically to see the formation's inherent orientation towards continual improvement. For the formations that have purely support roles viz. storage and despatch depots, ground training institutes, and repair depots, the first tier audit is not very sacrosanct in all the fields. Obviously, there is no environmental audit planned at this tier level.

The second tier audit process is more streamlined. It is carried out by a team specially deputed for the process from the regional HQ that controls the formation directly. The team members are not trained auditors but are chosen owing to their position at the HQ. This audit is a dedicated process and takes place in two to three days and, once again, the focus is on operational matters. It is almost on the same lines as the third tier audit but with one major difference. Mostly, the audit focusses on the processes that are linked to 'policy implementation' in nature. The policies by themselves are not being audited unless, of course, the formation being audited projects a strong reservation towards a particular policy issued by the HQ and, in that case, it is discussed and a further decision on its implementation is taken. This audit has great significance as it offers the formation an opportunity to highlight its weak as well as strong points directly to their controlling staff at HQ. It also offers a first-hand experience to the audit team members as to how the policies being formulated by them are affecting the working of the formation. This audit ordinarily takes place a few weeks prior to the third and top tier audit. It also checks the formation's preparedness for undergoing the highest level of audit.

The third tier audit of an IAF formation is a very detailed process. It is carried out by a team from the audit specialised directorate of the Service HQ at every formation, every one to two years. This team is specifically chosen for the process due to their professional abilities and comprises personnel from all fields of the IAF. Their mandate is the widest and requires them to audit even the policies (and obviously their compliance status) issued by Regional or Service HQ. Their audit spreads over almost a week. Each and every process, policy implementation, existing instructions based on these policies and related tasking, etc are all analysed by the team. This process does encompass some aspects of the environmental audit as it analyses a few aspects of implementation of resource efficiency policies. This is exemplified by the minute and meticulous maintenance process checks for conformity to the laid-down servicing schedules. Since the servicing schedules lay down the quantity of spares to be used for each activity, any variation should typically be discernible to a good auditor. Although the resource efficiency audits are limited in scope in the present form, they do lay a foundation for institutionalising a detailed environmental audit process within the organisation by using the existing infrastructure and resources.

In all the three tiers of audits, one major positive aspect that is given a high priority in any military organisation is the check on the morale of the troops. By extension, this implies that any issue which is likely to boost their morale is encouraged and the existence of a good environment in a formation is one such issue, as already explained in Chapter 2 on Waste Management. The audit agencies can actually be asked to expand their role, to undertake environmental audits as an extension of their existing audit exercise, as explained in the preceding two paragraphs.

Expanding the Scope: Methodology of Environmental Audits

For performing an environmental audit in a military organisation, the existence of two preconditions is a necessity. First and foremost, the organisation should have an environmental policy issued by the top echelon to rightly orient the audit agencies towards the larger picture. Without this orientation, the motivation of the auditors and operators alike would not be possible.[5] The policy would lay down broadly the expected environmental performance levels from the organisation and this can be then extrapolated for the individual units – the military formations.

The second important condition that needs to be met is the existence of benchmarks that would be used by the auditors for actually performing the audit. This sounds very innocuous and logical but is actually a tough task to achieve. Militaries have a penchant for secrecy, and rightly so, owing to the nature of their task. Another factor that has to be taken into account is the very different operating conditions of military formations owing to their varied geographical deployment patterns. Thus, generating a benchmark is a tough task, one without which the audit process cannot start. The methodology that can be adopted is to compare similarly placed and same hardware operating formations. The comparison figures would not be generally available as till now there was no need to generate or maintain these statistics. The process would have to start by issue of instructions by the central audit agency to record six monthly figures in the designated fields of activities. Only a few formations operating a similar type of hardware and operating in similar terrain may be used for comparison. Some amount of extrapolation may have to be resorted to in the incipient stages as it may not be possible to match all practices even in similarly placed formations. Then there may be cases where there is only a single formation operating that hardware or of that size. But there are many other indices that may be used for generating benchmark figures for a formation. The indices that may be used to generate approximate benchmark figures, could be the number of personnel in the formation, geographical size, number of vehicles, use of FOLs and operational use pattern of resources, etc. The important task is to start recording these statistics for all formations. A comparison of the benchmark figures of a formation (being developed for *inter se* comparison), on year-on-year basis, would itself reflect the trend of resource management practices being followed.

The audit agency would have to be careful to weed out 'benchmark biases'. These biases are those that can routinely creep in at any of the two stages as explained below. The formation undertaking the development of benchmarks knowingly, would tend to keep the 'targets achieved' figures low so as to be able to easily surpass them during the actual audit. In the same vein, the audit agency would need to safeguard against the tendency to overcorrect for these biases, knowing them to be present in some degree. This 'correction' would be based on the experience level of the auditors evaluating the benchmarks. It may also be useful to collaborate with the experts of a particular activity and his/her services may be coopted while developing the benchmarks.

The fields in which environmental audits are carried out have been mentioned earlier. The process to develop the benchmarks and to an extent perform the audits in these fields can now be explained. It should be appreciated that in all these areas, the benchmarks would be either the existence of a good practice itself or statistical figures that would indicate respect for resources and, thus, the environment. Therefore, showcasing the good practices and maintenance of commensurate records would be a common feature of all the processes undertaken to develop benchmarks for the environment.

A. Waste Generation and Disposal

- Existence of policies on industrial and municipal waste disposal at the formation level. Drafting the formation level policies from the ones issued by the higher formations (HQ) should be a standardised process and the audit authorities should aim for achieving standardisation in this process.
- Quantum of industrial waste **generation** per military hardware or equipment located in the formation. Record of all types of mineral FOL waste being generated as a ratio of these being issued for use, is another way of maintaining these records.
- Industrial waste disposal methodology – quantity **reused/recycled** as compared to that returned to the salvage depots. Recording of waste generated would be the first step in starting this process. The industrial waste disposal can also encompass the e-waste disposal systems.
- Compliance with municipal waste disposal laws – conservancy contracts and innovations. The requirement of incorporating a standard conservancy contract that does not contravene the waste disposal laws has been explained in the second chapter. How these contracts are

being enforced is another area that can be standardised throughout the organisation by the audit agency, once the benchmarks have been set.

B. FOL Usage for Mechanical Transport (MT)

- Maintenance of accurate data on MT and FOL usage in the formation.
- Quantum of MT usage/personnel in the formation. In a formation, the activities are standardised and, therefore, the MT usage should not show a large variation in general.
- Quantum of FOL spent/vehicles on strength. With the type of vehicles being the same in the military, these figures should be similar, allowing for minor variations.
- Innovative methodologies adopted, if any, for reduction in FOL consumption. This methodology would vary for each formation. It has been included in the benchmark tools so that the information on these innovations can be spread throughout the organisation through the positive feedback mechanism of the audit agency.
- Any reuse of resources activity being carried out in the formation. This reuse could be that of FOL, packaging material, and material resources, etc. The reuse has to be properly documented so as to be considered a standard practice.

C. Energy Consumption Patterns

This area is of major concern for the costs incurred and the saving potential that it offers. The figures available in the case the US DoD[6] indicate the attention that is paid to maintaining transparency in these affairs. It is another matter that not much progress is discernible even in the developed countries on this front, due to operational limitations[7]. Most of the progress is aimed at enhancing energy efficiency in buildings and utilities. This is one area where there is a large scope even in the Indian military. However, this does not fall under the purview of the responsibility of a formation in the field. These policies are made at higher levels and are implementated by the Military Engineering Services (MES) under the Indian Army, which provides civil engineering support to all the three Services in India. Thus, the audit agencies in each of the individual arms of the military (IAF/Indian Army/

Indian Navy) do not have much role to play in deciding upon the benchmark in energy efficiency in estate management. Since the MES has adopted the green building norms and is actively pursuing their implementation, the auditors can set their implementation as a benchmark in any new project that is being undertaken in the formation. This benchmark would be based on the availability/or lack of green procedures and designs for a particular utility in the operational or domestic area. This feedback would be useful for the authorities in Service HQ so that they can interact with the Engineering Services branch and exhort them to decide on cost saving green buildings in their domain.

Over and above what has been mentioned, there are areas wherein the energy saving orientation of a formation can be audited. It is possible if a comparison is made between two similar formations and within a formation (year-on-year basis) on the amount of power consumed in (a) operational areas; and in (b) domestic areas. The variations noticed in operational areas should be easily explainable being a function of the amount of operational activities undertaken (if not, then this would be cause for concern) but domestic consumption should show minor variations only. Any large variation should be accounted for through internal audits of the formation. These internal audit records should be maintained and available with the concerned staff in the formation. By and large, a rationale for these variations that is supported by proper documentation should be a welcome sign of the willingness of the formation to adhere to an energy efficiency regimen and should be seen in this spirit. This is because it may not always be possible for the military formation to really take measures on energy efficiency without proper sanctions from higher formations and mostly a lack of such forays would indicate dearth of proper directions from the top hierarchy rather than unwillingness on the part of the formation personnel. This audit would, thus, primarily highlight areas of policy and decision-making shortfalls. Benchmarks in this area would show the efficacy of policy-making and it would be the correct area wherein interaction with civil agencies like the Bureau of Energy Efficiency (BEE), etc can help in suggesting the roadmap for laying down concerted directions.

D. Environmental Friendly Orientation

Any organisation/formation can act on the environmental policies and legislations that are laid down by the authorities placed above it. The environmental audit would bring out the compliance status of the audited activities with respect to these policies/legislations. The requirement for the formation and the audit alike to go beyond mere compliance brings us to the domain of 'environmental orientation'. If the formation and its personnel possess this attribute, the environmental friendly activities would be a byproduct. Thus, it would be **desirable** (though not necessary) for any formation to showcase its environmental friendly attribute. To project this attribute and for the same to be checked by the auditor, is not an easy task considering there are no quantitative indices that would reflect this orientation.

Two benchmark activities or rather possessing the right values would reflect this orientation to a large extent. First and foremost, is the formation's willingness to study the impact of military activities on the environment. The second is the actual environmental training status of its leaders – the officer cadre. These two attributes are definitely not the only ones that would highlight the formation's willingness to go beyond compliance on environmental matters. However, these are the starting points in good environmental practices that go beyond merely complying with orders and instructions and, hence, should be treated as a must for developing their benchmarks. The thought process of 'beyond compliance' activities in a military formation would be explained to qualify this argument[8].

There are many simple activities that are carried out within a military installation that are necessary for operational preparedness and safety.

Box 3

Consider the act of spraying insecticide near the shoulders of aircraft operating areas to ensure that insects are eliminated so that birds are not attracted towards it and, thus, no harm is caused to the aircraft. This activity also needs to be studied from the angle of causing harm to the ground water/nearby water bodies depending upon the concentration of medicine used. It is not intended to stop the activity as a result of this study but to make it as safe as possible for the community that may be affected and, in this case, it would be the military personnel of the formation and their families. How this study is carried out and with what earnestness, viz involvement of experts, etc, would reflect the environmental orientation of the formation.

This act would go beyond merely complying with known good practices like 'plant more trees' or 'don't waste water', etc. Hypothetically, the end result in this case may be to continue the activity by changing the type of insecticide, but the formation would have set a benchmark in showcasing their environmental orientation for the other formations to emulate.

The previous chapter addresses the environmental training of military personnel. Considering the novelty of the issue within the military, it is imperative that training on the subject may be imparted as a part of basic training to the officer cadre in the first instance and going on for the other ranks subsequently. The audit agency always checks the training status of the officer cadre in a formation, considering it a basic requirement for operational preparedness. Similarly, the environmental training status of the officers on the posted strength would point out the direction that would be chartered by the formation on a subject not yet imbibed within the military ethos. Although the formation generally has minimum leverage on how many of the posted officers are trained/untrained, the result would highlight the need for policy level intervention for getting at least a few critical appointments trained on the subject. The decision on identification of such critical appointments that must possess domain knowledge of the subject is left to be taken by the higher echelons in the HQ. The audit agency can help the decision-makers in deciding upon the efficacy of the overall environmental training programme by comparing the orientation of formations with good and inadequate environmental training status of its personnel. Thus, this process would also help in auditing the environmental training programme till the process stabilises in the organisation. The feedback on training is also essential at least as long as it is in the initial phase of implementation.

While the benchmark on organisational environmental orientation may not result in a quantitative analysis, it is essential for finding out the policy deficiencies – lack of it or contextually, falling short of requirements. Therefore, their periodicity may be kept different from a normal audit. In the incipient stage of environmental policy formulation and implementation, these audits would be required more often, with a gradual stabilisation of periodicity.

E. Local Community Interaction

Another important aspect of an environmental audit is the amount of community interaction that takes place between the military leaders and the local civil community that stays in the vicinity. Since these two sets are not mutually exclusive, it is essential that their interaction is harmonious. The impact of military activities on the civil community and vice versa has to be understood and modified for compatible living. All the Air Force formations make it a point to educate the local community on the danger posed by birds to the aircraft flying in the vicinity. So activities like open municipal waste disposal that would attract birds are discouraged through active participation of the civil community. The military also has to play an equal part in modifying its activities to respect the community and not pose any danger to them. Understanding their concerns is the first requirement in achieving a healthy interaction. The process adopted to reach this stage may vary from one formation to another and, hence, laying a standard operating process may not work out. The presence of such a process – showcased through maintaining records of interaction – is the correct way of institutionalising the system. The benchmarks would be the level and frequency of interaction, harmonious relations achieved, and issues discussed/ resolved. Innovative approaches towards these interactions (if any) should be discussed in pan-organisational meetings.

F. Material Parsimony

Amongst all the activities that would be benchmarked for audit by the concerned agency, this happens to be the toughest to benchmark. It is because the military operates mostly in a standardised manner. Thus, the material inputs are all laid down and accounted for. Building material parsimony in such operating conditions and that too at the formation level, is a tough proposition. The way to go about it is to check the material inputs in those spheres of activities that are controlled by the formation (without policy level directives issued by HQ) and then compare it with a similar formation elsewhere. The material inputs in the activities that should usually be checked are those that are not specified in detail by a higher formation. For example, the use of packaging material in the logistics wing of the formation, use of paper in offices (through the paper bought or centrally received for the entire formation), and use of cleaning material purchased for the formation, etc. Many such activities can be set by the audit agency depending upon the type of formation being used for benchmarking.

While benchmarking these activities, it is also essential that the perspective of military readiness should not be lost. Material parsimony is not meant to degrade the military capability but rather to increase it by reducing its dependence on input resources. Hence, wherever the audit agency feels that corrective action is required to reduce the over-zealous use of the parsimony processes discussed here, they should not hesitate from recommending so.

Training the Auditors

By now, it must be clear to the readers that the auditors have an onerous responsibility on their shoulders, that of ensuring that an accurate feedback is available to the policy-makers. Environmental audits would require the auditors themselves to be well versed in the policies and the latest developments in the field so that when required, they are in a position to give suitable recommendations. Since this area is new for the military, most of the auditors would not have had the opportunity to fully acquaint themselves with the good practices that can be followed in this area by any military formation. Thus, there is no alternative but to conduct a capacity building abridged course for them before they can be entrusted with such audits. Module 4 of the training curriculum (Chapter 4) is considered apt for training the auditors. Considering the seniority of the auditors, the scope of the module may be enhanced or reduced (junior or senior respectively). It needs to be emphasised to them that this process is yet to stabilise in the military and, therefore, the need is to make the audit process corroborative rather than corrective in tenor. The training module should be so tailored that not only should it inform about the policies on the subject but also should focus on the practical implementation aspects as envisaged by the HQ. It should be made clear that one of the main objectives of following good environmental practices in the military is to build resource efficiency that would result in saving costs. Specific case studies may be used for training purposes with a caveat that generalisations are better avoided and right orientation is what needs to be developed first.

The issues that need to be specially covered are those that have been described above for the development of benchmarks. These are pertinent enough to warrant immediate attention and, thus, the auditors should be abreast of these issues and policies existing on the subject. During the training process, it may also be appropriate to involve civil experts in the field to understand the changes and advances that are being made in the relevant fields. There are many think-tanks also that can impart suitable information on the subject. Another way to build capacity on the subject is to involve the auditors in military-to-military exchanges in which such issues are on the agenda. To incorporate the environmental issues in military-to-military exchanges is another good practice that the top hierarchy has to kick-start in any military and the auditors need to make full use of the same.

Expected Outcomes

Enhancing the role of the audit agency should be with a purpose. The objectives of carrying out an environmental audit have been explained earlier in the chapter. Expected outcomes and milestones likely to be achieved by this audit also need to be understood so that a sense of purpose and closure is available to the auditors. These would now be explained.

- **Capacity Building:** The spirit of the environmental audit and its corroborative nature is expected to result in building the capacity of the organisation in understanding the nuances associated with environmental policies and their impact. For this to happen, it would be essential to communicate the findings of the audit in a transparent manner to the formation that had been audited. There would be many aspects that would have pan-organisation impact potential and they should, thus, be conveyed to all concerned through instructions by the HQ policy groups. Since the audit would also bring out the efficacy of the environmental training programme, it would help in refining and fine-tuning the same, thus, lending a hand in effective capacity building of the personnel.

- **Enhanced Organisational Efficiency:** Environmental audits would not be of much relevance in the military if they do not lead to enhanced organisational efficiency. For a win-win situation, it is essential that the audit process is easily able to highlight – and quantify – the areas that have shown enhanced efficiency. A compilation of feedback from audited formations would show how the benchmarks have been met (or not met) and sometimes crossed. The attendant benefits would be, thus, obvious to all concerned and lead to environmental forays with increased vigour.
- **Building Transparency and International Standing:** An additional advantage of environmental forays by the military is the positive image spin-off. The formation (and the organisation) manages to connect with a larger audience and leaves a positive impression of the work ethos. The country as a whole gains by this 'diplomatic offensive' by the military. The transparency of decision-making helps in motivating the troops as they see the larger picture of why a decision is being taken in a particular manner. The policy-makers also have more decision-making tools at their command and just like a doctor armed with all diagnostic reports, can make informed policies. More on the subject would be covered in a later chapter.
- **Positive Impact on the Environment:** Last but definitely not the least, the benefits accrued due to safeguarding the environment cannot be quantified. Safeguarding human security is a goal of any military and this is aptly fulfilled once the organisation undertakes active measures to ensure its actions are sustainable in the long run. An environmental audit helps to ensure that the policies of the organisation and their

implementation are in consonance with the larger role of safeguarding the environment. Thus, it plays a very important role in ensuring that the organisation as a whole follows a sustainable path to the future. This is a very coveted outcome of following a green policy and ensuring its efficacy through an environmental audit.

Total Environment Management: Willing Participation

Audit is not power. It should be seen as a knowledge sharing mechanism. This should be the underlying message that must emanate from each environmental audit activity. Environmental audits can only be started once the organisation has shown its 'green' intent through incorporating suitable policies, translating into implementable actions. The audits described here are meant to see the implementation process at the field formation level. While undertaking such checks, it is natural that certain aspects of policies would be held to debate and, thus, may lead to their refinement. This would imply that these audits would not be restricted to only ground level actions but would also lead to efficient policy-making.

On the whole, an environmental audit in the military would be performed by the internal agency that carries out the operational audit of formations. This would call for an increase in the scope of its activities. Since this type of audit is new for the auditors, they would need specific training to don the new mantle effectively. Their training programmes would need to be executed before starting the process. The activities that would be audited at the formation level are broad-based. Auditing these without any precedent would not be an easy task. For this, it is essential that benchmarks are established and used for measuring the performance of a formation. The process to benchmark these activities would also have to be carried out by the audit agency only so that they can establish the anchor points of these activities, which would be useful when they actually perform the audit of formations. It is expected that with environmental audits becoming a part and parcel of periodic audit activities, the organisation and environment alike would benefit from increased efficiency and reduced consumption of resources.

Notes

1. Case study on Programme Environmental Assessment in the US Army, http://aec.army.mil/usaec/nepa/asv-pea.pdf accessed on July 28, 2011.
2. http://aec.army.mil/usaec/newsroom/update/sum03/sum0305.html, accessed on September 14, 2011.
3. http://www.oag-bvg.gc.ca/internet/English/parl_cesd_200803_13_e_30139.html, accessed on September 15, 2011.
4. http://www.dtic.mil/dtic/tr/fulltext/u2/p010595.pdf, accessed on September 15, 2011.
5. For more on the environmental policy, please refer Manoj Kumar, *Environment Change and National Security* (New Delhi: Knowledge World, 2011).
6. http://www.cnsec.org/index.php?option=com_content&view=article&id=196:the-us-department-of-defense-valuing-energy-security&catid=96:content&Itemid=345 and http://www.dod.gov/ddre/doc/DoD_Energy_Security_Task_Force.pdf, accessed on October 2011.
7. http://www.energybulletin.net/node/29925, accessed on October 5, 2011, gives an analysis on how the DoD energy efficiency policies are not what it professes. Even this so-called negative image indicates how much data towards environment protection is maintained by one of the largest defence forces of the world.
8. Beyond compliance acts for good environment follow a slightly different logic in the case of the corporate world. For more on the issue, readers may wish to refer Neil Gunningham, ed., *Corporate Environment Responsibility* (US: Ashgate Publishing Limited, 2009), p. 297.

9

Diplomacy and Military: 'Talk the Walk'[1]

What a society sees in its armed forces is exactly what it asks for – no more, no less; what it asks for, tends to be a reflection of what it, the society, is. When a country looks at its fighting forces, it is looking in a mirror, the mirror is a true one, and the face that it sees, will be its own.

— Sir John Hackett, "The Profession of Arms"

Gone are the days when military and economic prowess alone could elevate any nation-state to the status of a superpower or a world hegemon. In the era of information revolution and public diplomacy, it is equally important for a nation to disseminate information in the public domain to build credibility; more importantly, legitimacy and transparency. With the advances in information and communication technologies, the task of publicising actions, along with generating readership for them, has become almost child's play. Image, reputation, rating at various indices – economic and human rights, to name a few – and credibility are now relevant public goods that have become prerequisites for steering a nation forward both domestically and internationally, primarily because a nation-state competes with not only other nation-states for these 'virtues' but also with the domestic constituents, including the non-governmental agencies, business enterprises as well as the civil society, as pointed out by Joseph S. Nye.[2] In this context, environmental diplomacy assumes significance in the 21st century due to concerns being expressed about environmental degradation. In fact, the industrialised world is putting pressure on the emerging economies such as India to be transparent about their environmental policies. At the national level, the need to highlight the actions being taken by different organs of the government in the direction of environment protection is extraordinary since the 'black hole strategy' will no longer serve 'national interest,' as capability – any capability – projection is now entwined with the 'power' status of a nation.

One of the most important entities of a nation-state's architecture is its military. Like any other organ of the government, the military too has environmental responsibility and accountability as it is a universally acknowledged fact that the armed forces are one of the biggest polluters in the world owing to the nature of their responsibility. Across the globe, especially in the developed countries, the military has been actively pursuing the task of creating visibility on the fight against environmental degradation within their countries or even at their deployed foreign location[3] – an action that can be termed as environmental diplomacy. In India, on the other hand, the political as well as military establishments are still lagging behind in terms of sending a similar message across to their own public and the international community at large. It has to be appreciated that the concept of diplomacy has evolved considerably and it now involves not only the policy-makers but also the public. The developed countries' military establishments have put their environmental orientation in the public domain, outlining the actions that form a part of their forays in this sector[4]. The span of activities covered under their environment/sustainability canvas is extremely large and normally put under the Environment Management System (EMS). An ISO 14001:2004 system of EMS[5] is a norm for the military in the US. ISO 14001 is the world standard for incorporating EMS in any organisation. As per the policy directive on their website, all formations of the US Army were supposed to be in compliance of ISO 14001 not later than financial year 2009. By placing such information in the public domain, the US Army achieves public admiration for the leadership displayed in this non-military domain. Of course, the tangential benefits that also accrue by such actions can be understood by keen strategists.

It has been found that the environment-friendly concerns of the armed forces in India are similar to those of the armed forces in the West in many ways. The disparity between the two is created by the lack of diplomatic efforts to highlight these concerns in the case of the former. Instead of restricting the military to a showground of adventure and patriotism only, one has to go beyond and also highlight the social role that they actively play. On the one hand, the existing gap between the military and civilian mindsets has to be bridged in order to address the issues of national security holistically. On the other, there is enough room for transparency at the level of social and environmental activities undertaken by the military, which have nothing to do with national security and, thus, there is no need to wrap them in the veil of secrecy. In India, the need to delineate the military from the polity has also been stressed upon from time to time to maintain its apolitical aura at all costs. The need of the hour is not to put the military on a higher pedestal but to demonstrate that its service is far more wide-ranging than is portrayed currently – sometimes negatively, with adverse connotations. An attempt would be made in this chapter to focus on ways that could be adopted to bridge this information gap and draw attention to the initiatives being undertaken by the armed forces in terms of environmental mitigation. An analysis of the reasons for such a weak approach towards environmental diplomacy and its negative impact would be made. Besides, it will also reflect on the ingredients of environmental diplomacy in the Indian context as well as its benefits for the armed forces.

Commitment: Deliver-and-Reveal Approach

The word 'commitment' is harped on by individuals and organisations in every sector. It is one thing to 'show' commitment and work towards it; it is a completely different thing to 'showcase' commitment (even while working towards it) and build confidence amongst the larger society. It is a well-established fact that environmental commitment is on top of the agenda of a majority of stakeholders in contemporary society. The corporate organisations seem to be ahead of the government agencies in their initiatives to prevent environmental degradation. The Corporate Responsibility for Environment Protection (CREP) has ensured that the same companies which were shown in a negative light due to their profit oriented practices, indulge in social service that could transform their image. Their situation is rather desperate for they understand the adverse impact potential of being seen in a negative light on the environment front when the common man and policy-makers alike are concerned about the looming global warming. Ironically, every department in, and affiliated to, the government has also been doing its bit to advance environment protection, but without a stated policy like the CREP. The only difference between the two is that the former have successfully trumpeted their achievements as an image-building exercise so that their business does not suffer while the latter are yet to publicise their work in the public domain in a comprehensive manner, due to a perceived lack of need. Most of the corporate organisations carry out well-designed and persuasive public relations exercises frequently using various means, including the media, while the government organs, including the military, have hardly shown any enthusiasm in engaging in such exercises. The situation in India borders on the ludicrous. The State Climate Change Action Plans (based on National Action Plans) displayed on the states' official websites are woefully short of information, are non-standardised and whatever information is provided, is not user friendly. There are exceptions here too; for example, the Gujarat state action plan is very well documented and correctly displayed. Such apathy actually does more harm than if the information was not mentioned at all.

It is an accepted fact that the armed forces have played a vital role in a plethora of humanitarian missions such as disaster management. The search and rescue missions in the aftermath of natural disasters like earthquakes and floods are quite familiar (as seen in the cases of the 2004 tsunami and the 2005 Jammu and Kashmir earthquake). However, the best illustration of the remarkable work being done by the Indian Army on the environmental front is its Ecological Task Forces (ETFs). The concept of ecological units of the Territorial Army came into force in India back in the 1980s and astonishingly, the Indian Army is the only army in the world to implement it. The ETFs are credited for the implementation of soil conservation projects in states like Uttarakhand, afforestation in Assam, Rajasthan, Jammu and Kashmir among other states, creation of Amarpura lake in Rajasthan, conversion of Mohangarh in Jaisalmer district into green fields, to name just a few. In fact, the ETFs are reported to have planted approximately two crore plants and reclaimed twenty-five mines in the past one decade.[6] The Indian Army Environment and Ecology Cell (IAEEC) is the central coordinating agency of all environmental and ecological activities undertaken by the Indian Army; these activities include afforestation and arboriculture, rainwater harvesting, wildlife and biodiversity conservation, use of renewable sources of energy, environment education and awareness, waste and wetland development, pollution control, and garbage management and waste disposal among others. The Army's efforts have fetched it recognition in the form of awards as well; some of them are – Indira Gandhi Paryavaran Puraskar (Highest Award for Environment), Green Governance Award by BNHS, Confederation of Indian Industry Green Award, Environment Conservation and Desert Development Special Award, etc.[7] It is, thus, surprising that with such active participation in environmental activities, this aspect of the Indian Army is not known amongst the Services, leave alone the civil population of the country. These ventures by the Army have been mentioned on its website but it is only recently that they have actively considered informing a larger audience through printed material. Col P.K. Gautam's work in this regard is noteworthy.

The active participation of the IAF in putting an end to emission of ODS while undertaking maintenance of aircraft as a part of the national commitment towards the Montreal Protocol, is significant. It has also been found through interactions with military officials that the IAF had adopted several villages, especially in the northeast and Jammu and Kashmir for providing a range of social services to the villagers, including education, healthcare, housing, sanitation and tree plantation among others. For instance, Air Mshl A. K. Singh (now retired) was awarded the Mahatma Gandhi Service Award in 2006 for his outstanding service to the people of Jammu and Kashmir after the catastrophic earthquake of 2005.[8] Most of these efforts go unnoticed as the need for following environmental diplomacy within the organs of government has still not been felt in India. If one looks at the pace at which countries like the US, Australia and the UK have gone about practising environmental diplomacy, India's position is dismal. For example, the carbon reducing projects run by the UK Ministry of Defence have got immense coverage the world over through the ministry's website. The Indian Army has taken the lead in terms of taking initiatives to highlight its achievements through its official website, but the other defence organisations and, most importantly, the Ministry of Defence (MoD) have not shown any inclination so far to publicise them with zeal and vigour.

Even the endeavours of the Indian Army go unnoticed by the general public due to lack of concerted efforts on the part of the MoD. Public diplomacy can prove to be more effective only if it is 'centralised' and 'collaborative', at the same time, projecting a coherent approach.

It is certain that in the well regimented system of the Indian military, this public diplomacy exercise would not work if the policy directives to the effect are not issued at the highest level. Additionally, to execute these policies at the grassroot level on a day-to-day basis, the personnel have to be aware and adequately trained in environmental matters. In fact, an EMS, its various elements being described in previous chapters, has to be set up by the Indian military before a public relations exercise can be launched to earn the respect of the common man. However, even now, a few aspects of the EMS are already in vogue in the Services but considering the military priority set, these are not being actively brought to the notice of the public. The Indian military need to focus on this aspect in its public discourses.

At a juncture when media attraction is relatively easier to obtain, the Indian defence establishment should be exploiting these readily available resources to garner support for its initiatives and create goodwill. Instead, the MoD has shown lack of enthusiasm to interact with the media. Surprisingly, the Indian MoD does not even have a highly visible spokesperson. Issues concerning national security should obviously not be exposed but there is no harm in showcasing the other side of the military – its social leadership – which is unknown to the common man as of now. This would change if the MoD were to adopt a policy on sustainability and safeguarding the environment. This policy then can be put on the MoD website and its implementation periodically updated. In fact, the implementation of the policy made on the EMS in the Indian military to the extent possible, considering the national security considerations, would actually transcend the current state of affairs even in the Western world. This can be the starting point for the three Services and other organisations (under the MoD) to make their own policies on the subject and showcase their implementation. Laying down an organisational hierarchy that would take care of this aspect of public relations would obviously need to be designed as different from the Public Relations Office (PRO) that exists for interacting with the media.

Environmental matters within the military have an overarching reach and, thus, need to be treated as much as a professional subject as others in the areas of operations, maintenance and administration.

As a well-reasoned strategy, the Departments of Defence in the Western countries have used their association with think-tanks to hold consultations on pertinent issues related to the environment and military and also release them for the public to take note of. For instance, the Development, Concepts and Doctrine Centre is a UK MoD think-tank that performs a range of tasks, including production of "concepts and doctrine," "forced migration', "informing decisions in defence strategy, capability development and operations," and "providing the foundation for joint education, both now and into the future."[9] This custom is absent in India as the association between our handful of think-tanks and the defence establishment is limited to small-scale consultations that are rarely highlighted. These are indications of lack of will to initiate diplomatic missions on the part of the Indian authorities handling defence matters. The youth in India is largely ignorant about strategic issues that are pertinent to national security and how the military is dealing with the larger security issues. There is a dire need to involve them through the aegis of these think-tanks so that these future leaders have a serious appreciation of the issues related to the country's security when they rise to be the policy-makers of tomorrow. This process can only start if the government accepts the role of defence think-tanks and consults them for policy formulations. This is happening in another organs of contemporary governance. The Indian Ministry of Environment and Forests actively involves various think-tanks/NGOs during the policy formulation and primary research work. Both sides gain valuable insight and mutual respect that is observed by the common man, giving birth to a positive environment. Therefore, there is no reason why the process cannot be emulated in the MoD.

Culture: Progressive or Regressive? A Challenge

What could these diplomatic failures be attributed to in the first place? The reason cannot be lack of resources or expertise as it does not require high-end technology. The answer is simple: culture. It is more important to realise that the need of the hour is not only to occupy the moral high-ground but to go one step ahead after the constructive results are achieved – to throw light on them. Culture has to be dynamic and progressive; disregard of diplomacy of any sort can only harm the cultural ethos of a country. In similar vein, the armed forces will end up harming themselves by neglecting environmental diplomacy. This is one subject that has the potential to immediately attract the people's attention as they are able to relate to the subject due to an information blitzkrieg on the subject already unleashed by the media – both print and electronic.

To put the 'cultural block' in a better perspective, one could look at the example of the Public Diplomacy Division of the Ministry of External Affairs. The need for having such a division was felt only in 2006 while the West had been dedicating considerable attention to this since World War II, especially during the Cold War, though under different tags such as Public Affairs. It was the event of 9/11 that altered the entire international political architecture and many countries in the West were forced to add more fuel to the public diplomacy efforts. In the case of India, the division became 'active' in the real sense only in 2009 when Ms. Nirupama Rao took over as the Foreign Secretary and decided to create online forums, blogs, facebook and twitter accounts, and so on. Regarding the armed forces, one can only wonder at the approach towards a predominantly public relations exercise of recruitment. In fact, advertisements for recruitment into the forces started barely a few years ago. Until then, the general public knew very little about them. So much so, that young aspirants could associate the IAF only with pilots; the presence of engineers, technicians and other staff in the organisation was (and to an extent, is) completely unknown to many. Therefore, one could conclude that advertising itself was a cultural shift. This was triggered by the drop in the number as well as the quality of the candidates applying for positions in the military. With the enforcement of the Right to Information Act (RTI) and an active judiciary, the second shift towards more transparency ensued. Due to this shift, the military personnel are now being trained to manage the RTI appropriately and effectively. The third shift has to manoeuvre the forces into the art of public diplomacy, which also includes environmental diplomacy. It has to be noted that the first two shifts were forced and reactive. The third shift should ideally be a proactive move. One could draw a parallel in this with India's foreign policy that had been dubbed by many experts as not only 'reactive' but also fence-sitting right from independence.

As far as military training is concerned, it leaves a void in the personnel's personal and professional lives by deliberately alienating them from burning social issues that affect them as much as they affect the common man. The roles and responsibilities of the military in the social arena are overlooked to such an extent that as soon as the personnel are exposed to the social milieu, they find themselves severely constrained. Right from their inception into the armed forces, they are exhorted to devote all their energy and resources – and some may say rightly so, towards issues of national security and war-fighting. The entire training process is so inward-centric that the military personnel are not provided any form of training in important areas like media management. The military officers cannot even interact freely with the media until they reach the top echelons of the forces. It can be said that they are groomed to be non-appreciative of social issues and as a result, there are no efforts being made to prepare the junior officers towards policies such as showcasing the environmental pursuits by the military. The leadership process that commences at the junior level and continues till the senior level, does not provide the requisite exposure to these social issues; at the senior level, they are required to work in tandem with the government functionaries all of a sudden, taking on a much bigger role than envisaged in their training or experience till then. This strategy followed right from the grassroots has resulted in the insulation of the defence organisations at the cost of losing out on many a 'diplomatic victory.' The media too refrains from focussing on the social and environmental leadership in the armed forces. They tend to stereotype the military in a fashion as ordained by the political leadership and, thus, refrain from ever contextualising social and environmental leadership with the military. There is a dire need for some out-of-the-box policies to pull out the junior military leaders from the cocoon of secrecy and national security and expose them to social issues so as to make them holistic leaders as they grow in service. Every military policy pertaining to social and environmental issues should be brought into the public forum and the media should be encouraged to give equal coverage to these aspects as much as to the war-fighting scenarios. The common perception that there is no relationship between the military and environment has to be discarded, within and without.

An All-Encompassing Reward-Reaping Exercise

The instruments of environmental diplomacy are based more or less on willingness. If this block is crossed, the diplomatic initiatives will follow. Any initiative which is implemented in the larger interest of the public must be showcased. It is true, unfortunately, that for this to materialise, the whole system which has been designed to be passive in terms of public relations and diplomacy has to be overhauled. Any systemic change could be executed through two approaches—top-down and bottom-up. The bottom-up approach could undeniably be an arduous journey as it goes against the military ethos. However, voices could be raised at the appropriate in-house forums allowed within the Services and the superior officers could be made cognisant of these concerns. The research community, media and civil society could also play their part in highlighting the benefits that would accrue to their military organisation if their visibility on matters of social importance is enhanced. The onus, however, lies on the top-down approach and policies have to originate from the top guard that would pervade all sections of the armed forces, irrespective of the positions of the military officers. It is imperative to define and assign the roles of these officers and not to estrange them from public view. The spin-off from these policies would encourage more people to join the armed forces, especially those who possess qualities of social or environmental leadership as also quest for adventure.

The benefits of environmental diplomacy are numerous. It has to be kept in mind that diplomatic initiatives serve the interests of the government, the military as well as the general public. First, if the MoD takes interest in launching such initiatives, they will reflect the efficient functioning of the government which would supplement its public diplomacy strategy besides enhancing credibility and integrity. Second, the emergent image of the government as a cohesive unit is expected to give confidence to the people about the nation's progress. The all-important 'connect' between the organs of the government and the people could help the former firmly hold the reins of power. Third, it would motivate the people to take up responsibility to work on environment issues as normally the armed forces are considered a community worth emulating. If, in an organisation, one person is in-charge of e-waste management and the other person is not aware of it, the overall benefits would not be felt. Similarly, the implementation of the government policies at the grassroots level would be facilitated by healthier public participation. It is a time-tested fact that any policy of the government, when implemented, can reap benefits in a sustained manner only if the public is kept attuned of these policies as well as involved in a full-fledged manner; this would ensure that the 'fruits' of the policy could be 'consumed' in the future too, irrespective of the various uncertainties associated with the establishment. What better way to motivate the citizens to work towards arresting environmental degradation than to show the military in the forefront for conveying such an important social message? Fourth, these initiatives would encourage the people to view the military organisations from a larger and better perspective. They would not only be motivated to join the armed forces, but take pride in visualising a balanced leadership that gives similar importance to social responsibilities as it does to national security.

There is an altogether different dimension to following an environmental diplomacy highroad within the military. In the recent past, India has been regarded as obstructionist in the international forum where climate change negotiations are being held. Showcasing of the military's commitment to work towards the overall national commitment of reducing energy intensity and increasing sustainability would only add to the nation's stature internationally. In the same vein, it may also be used as an agenda for international military-to-military exchanges. This subject, being an exercise for global good, provides ample opportunity for even competing militaries to interact and build bridges. Such exercises could, thus, be considered a step towards trust-building and confidence-building measures between countries. Furthermore, in the regional theatre, India could get leverage by sharing its expertise on environmental issues in regions such as South Asia and East Asia which are in India's immediate neighbourhood and, therefore, directly affect it. For example, this could form a part of regional organisations such as the South Asian Association for Regional Cooperation (SAARC) which has so far failed to integrate the region. Such an avenue can only be explored provided the policies on the subject are available for discussion and the personnel are aware of the same. As mentioned above, such a training programme on environmental matters is, thus, essential for the military personnel.

An operational reason for the military to highlight their commitment towards the environment would be for preparing their suppliers to supply green, thereby efficient, technology and products. Unless the military is ready to articulate succinctly what it wants from the intended products, the vendor would not customise them. To be able to say that a green product is required, would translate into lower dependency on resources, lower cost of operations, options for periodic upgradation, and necessitate a complete understanding of the dynamics of life cycle costing, including disposal costs. The important aspect of driving the green procurement drive within the military is a strong communication medium with the OEMs. The communication on green procurement can be optimised only if the military personnel possess the necessary experience of expressing their requirements in the language that is easily understandable by the common man. This again focusses on the dire need for the military to allow its personnel to debate and discuss important issues of the environment with civil leaders and expose them to the nuances of their thinking process on the subject. An inclusive thought process would indeed transform them into true leaders.

Take the Road not Taken

The country is currently witnessing an anti-establishment wave on account of several corruption exposés and inaction in the past year of 2010-11. This clearly reinforces the need for the government to adopt transparency as the supreme benchmark of governance and transparency can only be derived from sincere diplomacy. Diplomacy, on the other hand, should not be haphazard and it should be separated from propaganda for the sake of it, as much as possible. Propaganda can only further aggravate the existing tensions between the government and the civil society. The military also needs to 'reach out' to the larger public at a time when it has been pointed out to be callous by the human rights organisations. It is important for the people to know that the military is equally adept at handling human security that is mostly impinged by social and economic factors. It is the duty of the government agencies, including the military, to familiarise the public with the laudable tasks they accomplish in the social sphere, in a well-strategised manner.

The tradition of diplomacy that has always been one of the cornerstones of Western political thought, in both theory and practice, should be embraced in the Indian context. The time is ripe to get rid of the excess baggage that has prevented the country's progress to a great extent. The first step towards building expertise on any subject is to be aware of it completely. It must also be noted that the military should not only be 'committed' to social and environmental goals, but also be in a position to take mileage out of their efforts through measured diplomacy. Every military officer should be groomed to become a 'complete leader.' A truly civilised country is one in which the political class, the military and the civil society are appreciative of, and have trust in, each other. This trust can lead to synergy if the diplomatic efforts on both parts lead to better communication and understanding of common issues.

Notes

1. This chapter has been jointly written with Ms Dhanasree Jayaram.
2. Joseph S. Nye, "The New Public Diplomacy," *Project Syndicate*, February 10, 2010, see http://www.project-syndicate.org/commentary/nye79/English, accessed on July 8, 2011.
3. Air Mshl A. K. Singh (Retd), Wg Cdr Manoj Kumar and Atul Dagai, *Ozone Protection and National Security: A Military Perspective (Toolkit for Defence Forces)* (United Nations Environment Programme, Multilateral Fund for the Implementation of the Montreal Protocol and Centre for Air Power Studies (Nepal: Jagadamba Press, 2009), pp. 52-59.
4. US Army website http://www.sustainability.army.mil/ – shows how seriously they consider informing the public on sustainability programmes within their organisation, accessed on December 22, 2011.
5. For more information on ISO 14001, readers may refer http://www.iso.org/iso/

catalogue_detail?csnumber=31807, accessed on December, 2011.

6. P. K. Gautam, *Environmental Security: New Challenges and Role of Military* (New Delhi: Shipra Publications: Institute for Defence Studies and Analyses, 2008), pp. 26-28.
7. "Contribution of the Armed Forces Towards Conservation of Our Environment," see http://indianarmy.nic.in/Site/FormTemplete/frmTempSimple.aspx?MnId=Mn7z5DsNgvU=&ParentID=W4Xw5DL5GkM=, accessed on July 15, 2011.
8. "Modern Day Military and Effect of Climate Change," see http://airmarshalaksingh.blogspot.com/, accessed on July 8, 2011.
9. For more information, see http://www.mod.uk/defenceinternet/microsite/dcdc/, accessed on July 11, 2011.

Index